World War I
Primary Sources

World War I
Primary Sources

**Tom Pendergast
and Sara Pendergast**

Christine Slovey, Editor

GALE GROUP

™

THOMSON LEARNING

*Detroit • New York • San Diego • San Francisco
Boston • New Haven, Conn. • Waterville, Maine
London • Munich*

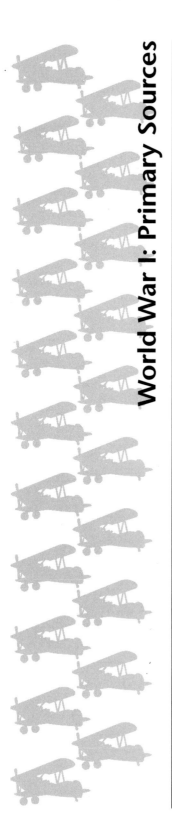

World War I: Primary Sources

Tom Pendergast and Sara Pendergast

Staff

Christine Slovey and Allison McNeill, *U•X•L Senior Editors*
Carol DeKane Nagel, *U•X•L Managing Editor*
Tom Romig, *U•X•L Publisher*

Pamela A.E. Galbreath, *Senior Art Director (Page design)*
Jennifer Wahi, *Art Director (Cover design)*

Shalice Shah-Caldwell, *Permissions Associate (Text and Images)*
Robyn Young, *Senior Editor, Image Acquisitions*
Pamela A. Reed, *Imaging Coordinator*
Dan Newell, *Imaging Specialist*

Rita Wimberly, *Senior Buyer*
Evi Seoud, *Assistant Manager, Composition Purchasing and Electronic Prepress*

Linda Mahoney, LM Design, *Typesetting*

Cover Photos: Rosa Luxemburg (Archive Photos. Reproduced by permission.); Ernest Hemingway (Corbis Corporation. Reproduced by permission.); Propaganda poster (Corbis Corporation. Reproduced by permission.); Germany surrenders (Corbis Corporation. Reproduced by permission.)

Library of Congress Cataloging-in-Publication Data

Pendergast, Tom.
  World War I primary sources / Tom Pendergast, Sara Pendergast.
    p.cm.
  Includes bibliographical references and index.
    Summary: Provides approximately thirty full or excerpted speeches, diary entries, novels, poems, correspondence, and artwork related to World War I, with information placing each in context.
  ISBN 0-7876-5478-7
    1. World War, 1914-1918--Sources--Juvenile literature. [1. World War, 1914-1918--Sources.] I. Title: World War One primary sources. II. Title: World War 1 primary sources. III. Pendergast, Sara. IV. Title.
  D522.7 .P38 2001
  940.3—dc21   2001053163

Contents

**An 1890s political cartoon
depicting the alliance
between France and Russia.**
*(Corbis Corporation.
Reproduced by permission.)*

**French and British soldiers
in a trench on the Western
Front.** *(Archive Photos.
Reproduced by permission.)*

Reader's Guide

W orld War I (1914–1918) was truly one of the most tragic events of the twentieth century. The war began over a terrorist act in the provinces of the fading Austro-Hungarian Empire and could have been avoided if Germany, Russia, and France hadn't felt compelled to obey secret treaties they had signed years before. Those secret treaties turned a small conflict into one that involved every major country in Europe and eventually many other nations from around the world. In the course of just over four years of war, nearly ten million soldiers and civilians lost their lives; billions of dollars were spent on killing machines—guns, tanks, submarines—and the economies of most of the warring countries were severely disrupted; two great empires, the Austro-Hungarian Empire and the Ottoman Empire, collapsed in defeat.

At the end of this terrible conflict, little had changed. Ethnic conflicts in the Balkan region continued to pit neighbor against neighbor. Attempts to create an international organization that would ensure world peace collapsed when America withdrew its support. Germany, though defeated, remained at odds with its rivals, France and England, and military leaders within Germany longed to avenge their defeat. Within twenty years of the end of World War I, these simmering tensions sparked another war, World War II, which returned death and destruction to the continent of Europe and to battlefields all over the world.

World War I: Primary Sources offers thirty-three full or excerpted documents, speeches, and literary works from the World War I era. Included are the "Dual Alliance" secret treaty between Germany and Austria-Hungary that set the stage for war; Woodrow Wilson's "Fourteen Points" speech, which became the outline for establishing peace at war's end; excerpts from Ernest Hemingway's *A Farewell to Arms,* a moving novel about one soldier's war experiences; and poems from leading war poets such as Wilfred Owen and Rupert Brooke. A sampling of World War I propaganda posters, as well as numerous first-person accounts from soldiers who lived through the horrors of battle, are also presented.

Format

The excerpts presented in *World War I: Primary Sources* are divided into five chapters. Each of the chapters focuses on a specific theme: A Soldier's Life; Documents of Diplomacy; America's Emergence As A World Power; Literature of the Great War; and The Home Front. Every chapter opens with an overview, followed by reprinted documents.

Each excerpt (or section of excerpts) includes the following additional material:

- An **introduction** places the document and its author in an historical context.

- **Things to remember while reading** offers readers important background information and directs them to central ideas in the text.

- **What happened next. . .** provides an account of subsequent events, both in the war and in the life of the author.

- **Did you know. . .** provides significant and interesting facts about the document, the author, or the events discussed.

- **For More Information** lists sources for more information on the author, the topic, or the document.

Other features of *World War I: Primary Sources* include numerous sidebar boxes, some focusing on the author of the featured document, others highlighting interesting, related information. More than fifty black-and-white images illustrate the text. In addition, a glossary runs alongside each primary document that defines terms, people, and ideas contained in the material. The volume begins with a timeline of events and a "Words to Know" section, and concludes with a subject index of people, places, and events discussed in *World War I: Primary Sources*.

World War I Reference Library

World War I: Primary Sources is only one component of a three-part U•X•L World War I Reference Library. The other two titles in this set are:

- *World War I: Almanac* (one volume) covers the war in twelve thematic chapters, each geared toward offering an understanding of a single element of the conflict; from the underlying causes of the war, to the many battles fought on the various fronts, to the anguished attempt to establish world peace at the war's end.

- *World War I: Biographies* (one volume) presents biographies of thirty men and women who were involved in World War I. Profiled are readily recognizable figures, such as U.S. president Woodrow Wilson and German leader Kaiser Wilhelm II, as well as lesser-known people like Jewish spy Sarah Aaronsohn and English nurse Edith Cavell.

- A cumulative index of all three titles in the U•X•L World War I Reference Library is also available.

Dedication

To our children, Conrad and Louisa.

Special Thanks

The authors would like to thank several people who have contributed to the creation of this book. We could ask for no better editor than Christine Slovey at U•X•L, who saw this book through most of its creation and always helped make our job easier. Dick Hetland—chair of the social studies department and teacher of twentieth-century American history at Snohomish High School in Snohomish, Washington—offered invaluable advice on how to shape the content of this book to fit the needs of students.

There are many others who contributed to this book without even knowing it. They are the historians and scholars who contributed their skills to writing books and articles on one of the most tragic events in human history. Their names can be found in the bibliographies of every chapter, and our debt to them is great.

Comments and Suggestions

We welcome your comments on *World War I: Primary Sources* and suggestions for other topics in history to consider. Please write: Editors, *World War I: Primary Sources,* U•X•L, 27500 Drake Road, Farmington Hills, Michigan, 48331-3535; call toll-free: 800-877-4253; fax to: 248-699-8097; or send e-mail via http://www.galegroup.com.

World War I Timeline

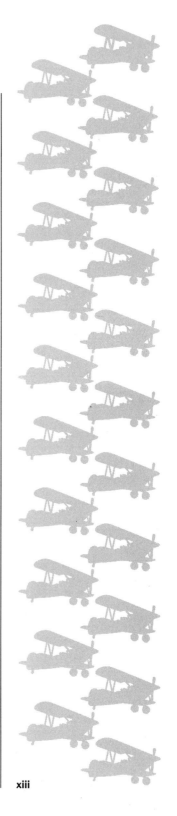

1871 German states unify after defeating France in 1870; this war is the source of some of the hatred between France and Germany.

1872 The emperors of Germany, Austria-Hungary, and Russia pledge their friendship to each other in the League of the Three Emperors.

1879 Germany and Austria-Hungary create the Dual Alliance.

1892 France and Russia create the Franco-Russian Alliance Military Convention.

1908 Austria-Hungary annexes (takes rule of) the provinces of Bosnia and Herzegovina, angering Serbia, which wanted to dominate the Balkan region.

1912 Dutch pilot Anthony Fokker establishes his airplane building company, Fokker Aeroplanbau, in Germany and gets his first contract to build planes for the German army in 1913.

1914 *June 28* Austrian Archduke Franz Ferdinand is assassinated by Serbian nationalist Gavrilo Princip in Sarajevo.

Germany's Wilhelm II and Emperor Franz Joseph.
(Corbis Corporation. Reproduced by permission.)

1914 *July 23* Austria-Hungary issues an ultimatum to Serbia to arrest and punish any Serbian official involved in the assassination; Serbia refuses to comply with its terms.

July 28 Austria-Hungary declares war on Serbia.

July 29–August 1 Kaiser Wilhelm II of Germany and Czar Nicholas II of Russia exchange a series of telegrams, known as the "Willy-Nicky Telegrams," in a last-ditch effort to avoid war between their two nations.

August 1 Germany declares war on Russia.

August 2 Germany makes a formal request to enter Belgium, a neutral country, known as the German Request for Free Passage through Belgium.

August 3 Belgium refuses Germany's request for free passage by pointing out that Germany is about to take actions that are morally wrong and illegal.

August 3 Germany declares war on France; German troops enter Belgium.

August 4 Great Britain declares war on Germany; Germany declares war on Belgium; United States declares its neutrality.

August 6 Austria-Hungary declares war on Russia; Serbia declares war on Germany.

August 10 France declares war on Austria-Hungary.

August 14 French and German troops clash in the Alsace-Lorraine region.

August 14 American poet Alan Seeger joins the French Foreign Legion in order to fight in the war.

August 16 Belgium surrenders its fortress at Liège.

August 19 Outlining his vision for the United States's remaining impartial during the war, President Woodrow Wilson delivers his "Declaration of Neutrality" speech before Congress.

September 5 A German submarine scores its first kill, sinking the British cruiser *Pathfinder*.

French reservists rushing to join the army at the start of World War I. *(Archive Photos. Reproduced by permission.)*

September 6-10 In the Battle of the Marne, the German advance into France is halted and Allied and German forces dig in to the trenches from which they will fight for the remainder of the war.

October 29 Turkey joins the Central Powers.

November 6 France and Great Britain declare war on Turkey.

1915 Rosa Luxemburg writes one of her most famous documents, *The Junius Pamphlet*, which discusses the impact of the war on working-class German citizens.

February 4 Germany declares a "war zone" around the British Isles, hoping to stop shipping to the island nation.

February 9 British and French begin assault on Gallipoli in Turkey.

March 11 Great Britain announces a blockade of German ports, hoping to starve the Germans of needed food and supplies.

April 22 Poison gas is used for the first time in the Second Battle of Ypres.

April 23 English poet Rupert Brooke, on his way to fight the Turks at Gallipoli, dies from blood poisoning before he sees any action in the war. His sonnets about the thrill of going off to war to fight for his country are very popular in England.

April 24 Turks begin massacre of Armenians.

April 26 France, Russia, Italy, and Great Britain conclude the secret treaty of London.

May 7 A German submarine sinks the British passenger liner *Lusitania*, killing 1,198 people, including 128 Americans. U.S. president Woodrow Wilson continues to proclaim American neutrality.

May 21 Dutch aviator Anthony Fokker perfects a mechanism to fire bullets through the spinning blades of an aircraft propeller; the mechanism becomes the standard on German warplanes and allows them to dominate the skies.

Rosa Luxemburg. *(Archive Photos. Reproduced by permission.)*

British pilots from the Royal Air Force. *(Archive Photos. Reproduced by permission.)*

May 23 Italy declares war on Austria-Hungary, honoring a secret treaty it had signed with the Allies.

June 6 German naval commanders order German submarines to stop sinking passenger ships.

June 9 U.S. president Wilson sends Germany a strong protest against Germany's use of submarine warfare.

September 1 Germany ends unrestricted submarine warfare, hoping to keep the United States from siding with the Allies.

September 6 Bulgaria joins the Central Powers, attacks Serbia.

October 6 Serbia is invaded by the Central Powers.

October 15 Great Britain declares war on Bulgaria.

October 23 Allied troops are evacuated from Gallipoli after being defeated by Turkish forces.

1916   *February 28* German forces in Cameroon surrender.

May 31 Naval Battle of Jutland.

April 24 The Easter Rebellion for Irish independence is crushed by British troops.

June 1-November 13 Battle of the Somme between Germans and Allies; the British use tanks for the first time in this battle on September 15.

June 4-September 30 Brusilov offensive, in which Russians attack Austro-Hungarian and German forces.

July 4 American poet Alan Seeger is killed in battle near the French village of Belloy-Santerre.

August 27 Romania enters the war on the side of the Allies.

August 27 Italy declares war on Germany.

September-November British forces march up Tigres-Euphrates valley, hoping to take Baghdad, but are defeated at Kut on April 29, 1917.

November 7 Woodrow Wilson is reelected as president of the United States; he campaigns on the pledge to keep the United States out of war.

An American nurse near the front. *(Archive Photos. Reproduced by permission.)*

1917 British army officer Siegfried Sassoon publishes his first collection of war poems, titled *The Old Huntsman.* His trilogy of autobiographical novels, *Memoirs of George Sherston,* is considered one of the best accounts of World War I.

February 1 Germans renew unrestricted submarine warfare.

February 3 The United States breaks off diplomatic relations with Germany.

February 23 Germans begin their withdrawal to the Hindenburg Line, a defensive position to the rear of the present front.

March 12 First revolution in Russia; Czar Nicholas II abdicates (gives up) his throne on March 15.

April 2 In the wake of recent events, U.S. president Woodrow Wilson delivers his "War Message" to Congress, explaining why he believes America should enter into the war.

April 6 The United States declares war on Germany.

April 16 Battle of the Aisne (also known as the Neville offensive) signals new French strategy, but the offensive fails within two weeks.

April 16 220,000 German workers stage peaceful strikes protesting the war.

June 25 First American troops arrive in France.

July 1-November 10 Third Battle of Ypres, or Passchendaele.

October 24 Italians defeated by combined German and Austrian forces at Caporetto.

November 4 British forces arrive in Italy.

November 7 Bolshevik forces seize power in Russia.

November 20 British use tanks effectively in Battle of Cambrai.

December 2 Fighting ends on Eastern Front.

December 7 United States declares war on Austria-Hungary.

December 15 Germans and Russians sign armistice; peace talks start a week later at Brest-Litovsk.

Czar Nicholas II of Russia, circa 1915. *(Archive Photos. Reproduced by permission.)*

The United States enters World War I, April 6, 1917. *(Corbis Corporation. Reproduced by permission.)*

A Red Cross ambulance at the Italian front.
(Corbis Corporation. Reproduced by permission.)

1918   *January 8* U.S. president Woodrow Wilson delivers "Fourteen Points" address before Congress.

April 28 Gavrilo Princip dies in the Theresienstadt prison in Austria.

March 3 Treaty of Brest-Litovsk signed between Germany and Russia.

March 21 Germans break through Allied front near the Somme, beginning their "Spring Offensives."

March 23-April 9 Germans shell the city of Paris.

May 7 Treaty of Bucharest ends fighting between Romania and Central Powers.

July 8 A volunteer ambulance driver for the American Red Cross, Ernest Hemingway is wounded during fighting on the Italian front.

July 15-18 Second Battle of the Marne, in which German forces begin to retreat.

July 18-August 15 Allied Aisne-Marne offensive.

August 8 Known as the "blackest day" for the German army, which was defeated in several key fights on this day and fell into a headlong retreat.

September 12-16 American offensive at Saint-Mihiel.

September 14 Allies begin assault on Germans and Austro-Hungarians along the Salonika Front in Greece.

September 25-27 Allies launch the Meuse-Argonne Offensive, the last major attack of the war and one in which American troops see significant action.

September 29 Bulgaria becomes the first of the Central Powers to surrender.

October 20 Germany abandons submarine warfare.

October 20 Turkey makes peace with the Allies.

October 29 German sailors mutiny against their commanders.

November 3 Austria-Hungary makes peace with the Allies.

November 4 Wilfred Owen, one of the greatest English war poets, was killed in battle one week before the end of the war.

German soldiers along the Western Front.
(Archive Photos. Reproduced by permission.)

November 9 Kaiser Wilhelm II abdicates (gives up) his throne; elected German officials declare the existence of the German Republic.

November 11 Germany signs armistice with the Allies, ending World War I.

November 21 German navy surrenders to the British.

1919 *January 4* Peace conference begins in Paris, France.

June 28 Treaty of Versailles signed.

November 19 U.S. Senate refuses to ratify Treaty of Versailles.

1921 *July 2* U.S. president Warren Harding signs a congressional joint resolution officially ending the war with Germany.

1929 Erich Maria Remarque publishes *All Quiet on the Western Front,* a fictional account of a young German soldier during World War I. It quickly becomes known as the greatest war novel of all time.

1929 Ernest Hemingway's famous war novel, *A Farewell to Arms,* is published in late 1929. It tells the story of an American ambulance driver who is injured while serving on the Italian front.

President Wilson campaigning to promote the Treaty of Versailles. *(Corbis Corporation. Reproduced by permission.)*

Words to Know

A

Allies: The nations who joined together to fight the Central Powers during World War I; they included France, Great Britain, Russia, Belgium, Italy, the United States, and several smaller countries.

Armistice: A temporary stop in fighting, or truce.

Artillery: Large-caliber weapons such as cannons and missile launchers that are capable of firing shells from a long distance.

Attrition: The gradual reduction in the strength of an army due to men being killed in battle.

B

Bolsheviks: A group of radical Russian activists who led the 1917 revolution in that country.

Bond: A certificate of debt issued by a government that promises repayment at a later date, plus interest; bonds were sold to raise money to support the war effort.

C

Campaign: A series of military operations undertaken to achieve a larger goal in war; a campaign will often consist of a number of battles.

Casualty: A soldier injured, killed, captured, or missing in the course of a battle; military strategists counted casualties as a way of assessing the damage done in a battle or campaign.

Cavalry: A military body that uses horses to move about the field of battle; after World War I, which saw the end of the use of horses in warfare, cavalry was used to refer to a mobile army force that used vehicles.

Central Powers: The nations who joined together to fight the Allies during World War I; they included Germany, Austria-Hungary, the Ottoman Empire (Turkey), and several smaller nations.

Chancellor: The leader of the German parliament, similar to a British prime minister.

Combatant: One who participates in a fight.

Conscription: Forced enrollment in the armed forces; often referred to as the draft.

Convoy: A group of ships sailing together in order to provide protection from submarine attacks.

D

Diplomacy: The practice of conducting international relations, including making treaties and alliances.

Dreadnought: A large, heavily armored warship.

E

Empire: A political unit consisting of several or many territories governed by a single supreme authority; before World War I, several of the combatant countries—including the Ottoman Empire, France, the United Kingdom, and the Austro-Hungarian Empire—were considered empires because they ruled distant colonies from their capitol.

Entente Cordiale: French for a "friendly understanding," this 1904 agreement between Britain and France promised cooperation in military affairs.

Exile: Enforced removal from one's native country.

F

Fascism: A system of government in which all authority—military, economic, and governmental—is held in the hands of a single ruler.

Flank: The side of a military formation; one army "flanked" another by attacking its side, where it was weakest.

Fleet: A group of warships under a single command.

Front: The front line of a combat force in battle; the point at which two armies meet.

G

Genocide: The organized extermination of an entire national, racial, political, or ethnic group.

I

Imperial: Having the characteristics of an empire.

Infantry: Foot soldiers; the majority of soldiers in an army, these soldiers are trained to fight and advance on foot.

Internationalism: The political belief that the world would be better off if all countries worked together to solve their problems; this was the opposite of "isolationism."

Isolationism: An American political viewpoint that held that Americans should avoid becoming involved, or "entangled," in European problems.

M

Matériel: Military equipment and supplies.

Mobilization: The act of organizing military forces in preparation for war.

Mortar: A portable cannon used to fire explosive shells at the enemy over a fairly short distance.

Mutiny: Open rebellion against authority.

N

Nationalism: Fervent commitment to one's nation.

Neutrality: An official government policy that declares that the country in question will not take sides in a war.

No-Man's-Land: The area between two armies, especially two armies fighting in trench warfare; No-Man's-Land could be as narrow as a hundred feet or as wide as a half a mile.

P

Parapet: An earthen embankment protecting soldiers from enemy fire.

Pogrom: An organized massacre or persecution of a minority group, often used to refer to the persecution of Jewish people.

R

Reformer: One who is committed to improving conditions, usually in politics or civic life.

Reparations: Cash payments for damages done during wartime.

S

Salient: A military term that describes a position held by one army that juts or bulges forward into the line of the other army. A military front without a salient is a straight line; one with a salient may have a variety of curvy shapes.

Shell-shock: A form of mental distress caused by coming under fire in battle.

Shrapnel: Fragments from an explosive shell.

Siege: A blockade placed around a town or armed fortress in order to defeat those inside it.

Sniper: A skilled marksman whose job is to shoot enemy soldiers from a concealed position.

T

Theater: A broad area in which military operations are conducted.

Treaty: A formal agreement between two countries.

W

Western front: Parallel lines of trenches stretching 475 miles between the Belgian coast and Switzerland. The majority of World War I was fought along the Western front.

World War I
Primary Sources

A Soldier's Life

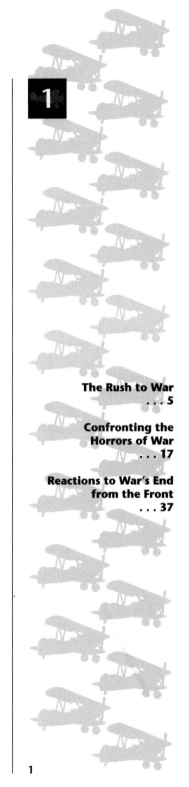

World War I, the conflict that engulfed Europe from 1914 to 1918, was triggered by the assassination of Archduke Franz Ferdinand (1863–1914) of Austria in June 1914. But this single event was not the only cause of the war; the seeds of war had been sown long before. Hungry to expand their territories or determined to maintain their possessions, countries had formed strategic alliances, aligning themselves against nations that appeared to be a threat to them. Armies had stockpiled weapons, and military leaders had drawn up elaborate plans of attack. Soon after the fatal shot struck Franz Ferdinand, citizens across the globe were rallied by calls to serve in the war effort.

In the beginning, no one knew that World War I, also called the Great War, would change warfare forever. No one knew that the powerful artillery, the machine guns, and the other advances in weaponry would slaughter eight million young men and soak battlefields in blood. No one knew that the carnage would last for four years, almost destroying an entire generation of young men. And no one knew that the horror of such a war would destroy many people's confidence in the goodness of the human race.

Prior to the outbreak of World War I, Europe had lived in relative peace for a hundred years, excepting the Crimean War (1854–56; a war that pitted Russia against Turkey, England, France, and Sardinia) and the Franco-Prussian War (1870–71; a war between France and the Germanic states, the strongest of which were Austria and Prussia). There had not been a general European war since the defeat of Napoléon at Waterloo in 1815. And the world had only known wars to be rather quick and not too bloody. When the war began, many thought it would be over in six months.

At first, citizens across the world enthusiastically supported their countries. Men raced to sign up for military service, eager to get involved before the action would be over. New recruits marched off to war cheered by crowds of well-wishers. Anywhere a crowd would gather, be it a soccer match or a church service, military recruiters could be found, signing up young men—and later, women—to serve their countries.

Though many soldiers marched off to the sound of bands playing patriotic songs and wildly cheering crowds, they did not achieve the quick results the enthusiastic crowds hoped for. Instead, soldiers found themselves embroiled in a deadly conflict, the likes of which they had never imagined possible. Soldiers were stuck in a nightmarish stalemate at the Western Front. In attempts to win the war, each side in turn made the war worse, either by including more people—as when the Allies opened new fronts against the Austrians in the Swiss Alps and along the Isonzo River in 1915, or when the British invaded Gallipoli that same year—or by creating more destructive weapons—like poisonous gas, which the Germans introduced in 1915, and the tank, which the British introduced in 1916.

Besides changing the practice of warfare, World War I changed the lives of many people. During the war, soldiers' experiences were recorded in the letters they sent to loved ones at home, in diaries, and in poems. After the war, people published memories of the war in autobiographies, histories, and fiction. The names of those who captured the war experience with great literary skill are well known; they include soldiers such as Wilfred Owen, Siegfried Sassoon, and Ernest Hemingway. You can read about their experiences in chapter 4, Literature of the Great War. Others, faceless millions, wrote too.

They recorded their surprise, their horror, their despair, their wonder, and their pride in brief notes and rambling letters. Their words create a picture of the war like no other, a picture of how four years of war changed people's ideas about war and about life. This chapter gives you a glimpse into the thoughts and experiences of these people through samples of their letters, diaries, and autobiographies. **The Rush to War** highlights the experiences of a variety of men as they entered military service and includes excerpts from *1914–1918: Voices and Images of the Great War; The First World War: An Eyewitness History;* and *Some Desperate Glory: The World War I Diary of a British Officer, 1917.* **Confronting the Horrors of War** presents soldiers' reactions to combat and includes excerpts from *1914–1918: Voices and Images of the Great War; Good-Bye to All That; Sagittarius Rising;* and *The First World War: An Eyewitness History.* **Reactions to War's End from the Front,** with excerpts from *Lines of Fire: Women Writers of World War I; The Storm of Steel: From the Diary of a German Storm-Troop Officer on the Western Front;* and *1914–1918: Voices and Images of the Great War,* illustrates the variety of reactions that people on the front had to news about the war's end.

The Rush to War

Excerpts from 1914–1918: Voices and Images of the Great War

Edited by Lyn Macdonald
Published in 1988

Excerpt from The First World War: An Eyewitness History

Edited by Joe H. Kirchberger
Published in 1992

Excerpt from Some Desperate Glory:
The World War I Diary of a British Officer, 1917

By Edwin Campion Vaughan
Published in 1981

Upon the declaration of war, citizens from every country gathered to unite against their new foes. Fueled by patriotic fervor, the crowds grew seemingly hysterical with nationalistic feelings. French ambassador to Russia Maurice Paléogue labeled the beginning of the war "world madness," according to W. Bruce Lincoln in *Passage through Armageddon: The Russians in War and Revolution 1914–1918.*

Two days after Germany's declaration of war on August 4, 1914, angry Russians displayed their patriotism by ransacking the German embassy in St. Petersburg. The czar (leader of Russia) and Russian military leaders worked to unite the Russian people against the Central Powers (the countries united behind Germany and Austria-Hungary, fighting against the Allies). Russians responded quickly. Many Russians had no idea that Germany existed as a country, and they cared little for politics or conflicts outside their motherland; still, hundreds of thousands of Russians marched off to defend their country. Czarina Alexandra remarked that the war "lifted up spirits, cleansed the many stagnant minds, brought unity in feelings, and was a 'healthy' war in the moral sense," as quoted by Lincoln in *Passage through Armageddon.*

"I sank back into the cushions, and tried to realize that, at last I was actually on my way to France, to war and excitement—to death or glory, or both."

From Some Desperate Glory: The World War I Diary of a British Officer, 1917

Recruiting posters such as this encouraged many men to enlist for military service. *(Archive Photos. Reproduced by permission.)*

"SUB SPOTTED—
LET 'EM HAVE IT!"

LEND A HAND—Enlist in your Navy today

Citizens of other nations also greeted the war with optimism and hope. Men signed up eagerly for the war, and crowds cheered them with hopeful cries for victory. People across the world knew that the war had been brewing for years, and they hoped that the armed conflict would quickly bring a lasting peace. In France, the departure of troop trains to the front occurred in an atmosphere of celebration. A French soldier quoted in John Keegan's *The First World War* remembered the scene:

At six in the morning, without any signal, the train slowly steamed out of the station. At that moment, quite spontaneously, like a smouldering fire suddenly erupting into roaring flames, an immense clamour arose as the Marseillaise *[a French anthem] burst from a thousand throats. All the men were standing at the train's windows, waving their kepis [caps]. From the track, quais [loading docks] and the neighbouring trains, the crowds waved back. . . . Crowds gathered at every station, behind every barrier, and at every window along the road. Cries of "Vive la France! Vive l'armée" ["Long live France! Long live the army"] could be heard everywhere, while people waved handkerchiefs and hats. The women were throwing kisses and heaped flowers on our convoy. The young men were shouting: "Au revoir! A bientôt!" ["Goodbye! See you soon!"]*

After the initial call to arms, recruiting efforts continued. Sporting events became opportunities to recruit from the stands. Crowds would sing patriotic songs to stir spectators into enlisting. Recruiting posters also encouraged many to enlist and helped each country supply the front with fresh soldiers. British posters, which secured the enlistment of an estimated one-quarter of all British soldiers, read: "Your Country Wants You" and "Women of Britain say, GO." After the sinking of the British passenger ship *Lusitania* by a German submarine, an Irish poster rallied men to fight: "Irishmen Avenge *The Lusitania.* Join an Irish Regiment To-Day." The most famous French poster relied on France's pride in the fighting spirit of its troops. Showing an eager soldier charging forward, the poster read "We'll get them!" A German poster of a soldier with shining, determined eyes beckoned young men to "Help us win!" In America, recruiting posters read "It's up to you. Protect the nation's honor." (*See* Chapter 5 for more examples of World War I recruiting and propaganda posters.)

The men who signed up never imagined that the war would drag on for four years. In every nation, writes Lincoln, the "youth marched off to war expecting adventure and glory, not suffering and death." The following excerpts indicate the enthusiasm and confusion of the times. They also reflect the innocence of the enlistees. Taken from the diaries of soldiers or from autobiographies written years after the war, the excerpts offer a snapshot view of men's feelings about leaving for war. The full details of these men's lives are not available, but these small samples of their writings illustrate the variety of responses that men had to enlisting.

French reservists rushing to join the army at the start of **World War I.** *(Archive Photos. Reproduced by permission.)*

Things to remember while reading the personal stories of enlisting:

- France, Russia, and Germany used universal conscription or required service, also called the draft, to create their huge armies. The United Kingdom relied on volunteers to fill its army but later also used a draft.

- Russia, with its vast population, had the largest army of any combatant. Russia's peacetime strength (the number of soldiers in active service ready for battle) stood at 1,445,000 in 1914; Russia was capable of increasing this force to 3,400,000 in case of war, according to statistics quoted by Niall Ferguson in *The Pity of War.*

- France followed Russia in peacetime strength, with 827,000 soldiers, a force it could increase to 1,800,000 in wartime.

- By 1914, according to statistics cited by Ferguson, the German military had a peacetime strength of 761,000 men and was capable of increasing that number to a wartime strength of 2,147,000.

Excerpt from 1914–1918: Voices and Images of the Great War

Private Carson Stewart

7th (S) Battalion, Queen's Own Cameron Highlanders (Scottish)

I enlisted in the Queen's Own Cameron Highlanders on 9 September, 1914 at the Institute in Cambuslang. I really did not go up to the Institute with the intention of joining up. I just went up to see the fun of others joining up, because whenever a lad went in to join up, the crowd outside would give him a hearty cheer. So after standing around for a while I must have got carried away. So in went another recruit—me! I was duly sworn in and became a Soldier of the King in the Queen's Own Cameron Highlanders.

*I was given a **Railway Warrant** to report to the Barracks at Inverness. Well do I remember arriving at the Barracks late at night about 14 September. In the morning I, along with the other new recruits, was paraded to give our particulars to an **NCO**: age, trade, place of birth etc. Then we were given a Regimental number. My number was 13013. Now, I ask you, with a number like that, what a start to my Army Career!*

*So many new lads were joining up that they could not cope with the rush, no uniform to be had. So we just had to parade in our civilian clothes that we had arrived in. The first day on Parade was a bit of a laugh, as the new boys were a very mixed lot, small ones, big ones, students 'tough guys' and some of the very Gentleman Type, and if you left anything down, then the 'Scruff Class' soon got their fingers on it, especially a watch or a good **shaving outfit.***

*While I was in Inverness Hospital, the result of a kick playing football, I saw some queer tricks played by the soldiers, especially the **old soldiers**, the **Regulars** who had come home from abroad and who were acting the **fly men**. They used to swallow a bit of **cordite** taken from a bullet, so their heart would go pitter-patter when they were being examined by the doctor, and some of the cute boys rubbed their eyes with an onion to make them water and run. **They were up to all the tricks.** One lad was having a bad time by the injections he was having—the result of his going with dirty women. He used to faint when having the treatment. It made me scared to look at a girl.*

Railway warrant: Railway ticket issued by the military.

NCO: Noncommissioned officer, such as a sergeant or corporal.

Shaving outfit: Kit of shaving supplies.

Old Soldier: A soldier experienced at avoiding military duty.

Regulars: Army soldiers.

Fly men: Slang for smart aleck.

Cordite: An explosive powder.

They were up to all the tricks: Soldiers tried a variety of ploys to pretend to be too ill to be sent back to the front.

Owing to the large number of new recruits arriving at Inverness, we were transferred to Invergordon, where we joined thousands of other Camerons of the 3rd Feeding Battalion. We had to sleep in bell tents in a huge field about fifteen men to each tent (too many). Then wet weather set in and our civilian clothes were in an awful mess. I looked **a proper Charlie** with my cap down over my eyes at times, as the **skip** was broken.

A problem at Invergordon was the sanitary arrangements. One had to go some distance to the end of the field to the **WC**, and sometimes the soldiers had a bet on—would he make it, or not? It was a big advantage when we got issued with **kilts.** It was a good laugh to watch the boys running to the WC.

The weather continued to be bad with food very poor. Under such conditions some of the boys volunteered for France, thinking the trenches could not be so bad, but they soon found out that the trenches were worse then [than] Invergordon—a whole lot worse. Some of the young lads had only about two or three months training before being sent to France.

One of the first boys to go to France was Private Day. He was killed at Festubert on 9 May, 1915, in a grim battle that cost the Scots many lives. Another lad, Private Phillips, was wounded at Festubert. He was lucky to get home to Glasgow where I visited him in hospital. He told me to be sure to take my running shoes to France as you had to **Get off your Mark at the Double.** He scared the life out of me! [Macdonald, pp. 27–28]

Excerpt from The First World War: An Eyewitness History

André Fribourg

French 106th Regiment soldier

Our hearts beat with enthusiasm. A kind of intoxication takes possession of us. My muscles and arteries tingle with happy strength. The spirit is contagious. Along the line track walkers wave to us. Women hold up their children. We are carried away by the greeting of the land, the mystery that the future holds, the thought of glorious adventure, and the pride of being chosen to share it. [Kirchberger]

A proper Charlie: A fool.

Skip: Brim of a hat.

WC: Water closet; latrine.

Kilts: Knee-length skirts worn by Scottish men.

Get off your Mark at the Double: Move quickly.

Excerpt from 1914–1918:
Voices and Images of the Great War

Joseph Murray

British Able Seaman, Hood Battalion,
Royal Naval Division

I left on the midnight train from Newcastle for King's Cross and believe me there was more people outside the train than inside the train when the damned thing moved off. People saying 'Goodbye,' some of the lassies hugging each other, Mums crying, it was dreadful. Anyhow, we got to King's Cross at six o'clock in the morning. We got off the train in a heap and the old Petty Officer, Charlie Sammes, he came out.

'Fall in here!' 'Come on, Straighten up!' 'What do you mean by "fall in?"' We knew nothing about training, no idea at all. 'Number!' 'What the Hell's that?' we wondered. 'One, two, three, four!' We had half a dozen go's at this numbering business. I thought to myself, 'Now, it's simple enough, I don't know what they want the numbers for, but it's simple enough.' I was Number 13, I was Number 12 the first time, but I thought, 'Well, sod that for a tale, I don't want to be Number 13 to start the War.' I started pushing back and we started numbering again and I'm back at twelve. The Petty Officer came along, 'Now, we'll do it again, shall we?'

He got us lined up and he said, 'Form Fours! What I want you to do is the outer numbers take a pace to the rear with the left foot and the others to the right and then stand still. All right, go on!' I didn't know whether I had to move or not. Some of them didn't know what to do, some of them moved off on the wrong foot. Really and truly, it was comical. Anyhow, he got us into four ranks eventually. 'Form Fours! Right, that's better, do it again! Form Fours! Fine! Now, when I say, "Move," get back in the train!' I thought to myself, 'Where the Hell are we going to now?' He said, 'Move,' and we all get back into the train again. 'Now,' he says, 'we'll have it done properly. Disembark!' So we all clambered out—perfect. I thought to myself, 'We're not going to get to the War, we're going to spend the rest of the War on Platform Six at King's Cross!' [Macdonald, p. 28]

Sod: A curse meaning roughly "Darn."

Excerpt from Some Desperate Glory: The World War I Diary of a British Officer, 1917

Edwin Campion Vaughan
British Second Lieutenant

January 4, 1917

It was an incredible moment—long dreamed of—when the train steamed slowly out of Waterloo, a long triple row of happy, excited faces protruding from carriage windows, passing those which bravely tried to smile back at us—we were wrapped in the sense of adventure to come, they could look forward only to loneliness. We took a last long look at the sea of faces and waving handkerchiefs—and we left.

When we had swept round the bend, away from the crowded platform, ringing with farewell cheers, I sank back into the cushions, and tried to realize that, at last I was actually on my way to France, to war and excitement—to death or glory, or both. [Vaughan, p. 1]

What happened next . . .

Each country was convinced that it needed millions of soldiers in order to win the war. After the first groups of soldiers left for the front, governments began churning out propaganda (materials aimed at convincing people of an idea) to persuade more men to join and serve. The propaganda came in several forms: Recruiting posters depicted the enemy as a menace that must be quashed; newspaper reports detailed the atrocities committed by the enemy; censorship of the press helped governments shape the opinions of citizens and persuaded many men and women to sign up to serve in the armed forces.

As they gained soldiers, armies needed to move those troops quickly and efficiently. Before 1914, military strategists in many countries had developed elaborate plans for mobilizing troops in time of war. In the beginning weeks of the war, countless trains were scheduled to leave at specified intervals to whisk soldiers from German cities to the border of Belgium. In France, traffic backed up for mile after mile on eastbound roads heading toward the front. In Russia, soldiers came to

serve their country from more than eight million square miles of territory, but because of Russia's small railway network, their travel was slower than soldiers' travel elsewhere.

As the war wore on, governments continued to persuade more and more people to enlist. But the men and women who joined after 1914 did not leave with the same innocence as the first troops to fight at the front. Guy Chapman joined the British army in 1915; he put his thoughts bluntly in his memoir, *A Passionate Prodigality*:

> "I was **loath** to go. I had no romantic illusions. I was not eager, or even resigned to self-sacrifice, and my heart gave back no answering throb to the thought of England. In fact I was very much afraid; and again, afraid of being afraid, anxious lest I should show it."

The crowds seeing the soldiers off were also changed as the war's casualties started filling hospitals and as civilian women and men struggled to bring in the crops and keep the factories working without their nation's strongest and most able-bodied men.

U.S. soldiers departing for World War I are sent off with enthusiasm. As the war progressed, however, enthusiasm waned.
(Corbis Corporation. Reproduced by permission.)

Loath: Not willing; reluctant.

Did you know . . .

- Together, the Central Powers could count on a wartime army of 3,485,000 men—over two million men less than the Allies in 1914.

- In May 1917, the Selective Service administration began registering for the draft all American men between the ages of twenty-one and thirty.

- Although sheer numbers of soldiers were a top priority to military strategists, the ability to mobilize (move troops to a battlefield) was another crucial element to success. In 1914 Germany had the most advanced railway system in Europe, which meant that it could quickly move troops to battle.

- Unlike Germany, France, England, and Austria-Hungary, which could mobilize their armies within days, Russia did not expect to be fully mobilized for three months.

- Some Frenchmen used taxis to travel to the front.

- Unable to convince enough people to enlist voluntarily, the United Kingdom passed a conscription law in 1916. The law obliged single men between ages eighteen and forty-one to serve in the military.

For More Information

Books

Chapman, Guy. *A Passionate Prodigality*. 1933; London: Buchan and Enright, 1985.

Ferguson, Niall. *The Pity of War: Explaining World War I*. New York: Viking, 1998.

Fribourg, André. *The Flaming Crucible: The Faith of the Fighting Men*. Trans. Arthur B. Maurice. New York: Macmillan, 1918.

Keegan, John. *The First World War*. New York: Alfred A. Knopf, 1999.

Kirchberger, Joe H., ed. *The First World War: An Eyewitness History*. New York: Facts on File, 1992.

Lincoln, W. Bruce. *Passage through Armageddon: The Russians in War and Revolution 1914–1918*. New York: Simon and Schuster, 1986.

Macdonald, Lyn. *1914–1918: Voices and Images of the Great War*. London: Michael Joseph, 1988.

Vaughan, Edwin Campion. *Some Desperate Glory: The World War I Diary of a British Officer, 1917*. New York: Henry Holt and Company, 1981.

Web sites

BBC News: The Great War on Eighty Years. [Online] http://news.bbc.co.uk/ hi/english/special_report/1998/10/98/world_war_i/newsid_197000/ 197437.stm (accessed March 2001).

The Great War and the Shaping of the Twentieth Century. [Online] http://www.pbs.org/greatwar (accessed October 2000).

The 1918 Influenza. [Online] http://www.library.utoronto.ca/spanishflu/ 1918.html (accessed December 2000).

World War I: Trenches on the Web. [Online] http://www.worldwar1.com (accessed October 2000).

Confronting the Horrors of War

Excerpts from 1914–1918: Voices and Images of the Great War

Edited by Lyn Macdonald
Published in 1988

Excerpt from Good-bye to All That

By Robert Graves
Published in 1957

Excerpt from Sagittarius Rising

By Cecil Lewis
Published in 1936

Excerpt from The Storm of Steel: From the Diary of a German Storm-Troop Officer on the Western Front

By Ernst Jünger
Published in 1929

By the end of 1914 it was clear that World War I was unlike any war that had come before it. The powerful artillery and machine-gun fire proved more devastating than anyone had imagined possible. French, German, and English forces suffered terribly—90 percent of the British Expeditionary Force were casualties (seriously wounded or killed) in 1914.

The early battles resulted in a stalemate. Opposing forces dug deep trenches into the earth; from the trenches soldiers could safely lob explosives at their enemies. The majority of the war was fought from parallel lines of trenches stretching 475 miles between the Belgian coast and Switzerland. This line was called the Western Front. Both the Central Powers and the Allies dug complicated networks of first-, second-, and third-line trenches connected by supply and communication trenches. The Germans dug elaborate, well-engineered trenches—some even included plumbing—while the Allied forces chiseled out crude dugouts that were decidedly less accommodating. Both sides positioned machine guns in frontline trenches to prevent

"When nothing happened I opened my eyes and saw, to my immense relief, a large shell half buried in the earth only one and a half metres away from me. It was a dud. Thus we waited in our holes for ten hours—the most fearful ten hours I had ever experienced in my life."

Sergeant Gottfried Kreibohm

French and British soldiers in a trench on the Western Front. *(Archive Photos. Reproduced by permission.)*

advances and along second- and third-line trenches to cover any breakthroughs. Each line of trenches was protected by tangles of barbed wire, which guarded against any advancing soldiers who managed to cross the barren stretch of land called no-man's-land between the opposing trenches.

Trenches changed army life. Instead of relying on the daring hand-to-hand combat that had won previous wars, soldiers of World War I lobbed explosives at each other from deep dirt holes. Through curtains of shell-fire, soldiers witnessed unimaginable destruction; the blood of hundreds of thousands of their comrades soaked the fields that separated them from their enemy; heavy artillery ripped huge holes in the earth and could bury men alive. Sitting in their damp, stinking, dirt trenches, soldiers lurked, fearful of peering over the top. And as the war dragged on, the supplies to the front and the numbers of replacements dwindled, leaving tired, hungry soldiers to hold the front.

The following excerpts are samples of the diaries and autobiographies of soldiers from both sides. Their notes describe what it was like to be a soldier—living in a trench, flying a reconnaissance (information-gathering) mission, surviving a near miss, helping the wounded, seeing death all around, working when tired and hungry, fearing the enemy, conquering their fear, and feeling proud. Little is known about the lives of many of the individuals who wrote these excerpts, but their writings paint a vivid picture of the war from a soldier's perspective.

German troops attacking across no-man's-land, the stretch of land between opposing troops' trenches. *(Archive Photos. Reproduced by permission.)*

Things to remember while reading the personal stories of fighting:

- The author of the second excerpt, Robert Graves, enlisted a few days after England declared war on Germany, partly as a way to delay his entrance to Oxford University, which he dreaded.

- The author of the fourth excerpt, Cecil Lewis, signed up for service in the Royal Flying Corps in England because, being under seventeen, he was too young to join the regular army corps.

- The author of the last excerpt, Ernst Jünger, joined the German army during the first year of the conflict, at age nineteen.

- No personal information is known about the soldiers who wrote the other passages.

Excerpt from 1914–1918: Voices and Images of the Great War

Private W. Hay
The Royal Scots, 1st/9th Battalion (Scottish)

[1916 — Battle of the Somme]

*You were between the devil and the deep blue sea. If you go forward, you'll likely be shot, if you go back you'll be court-martialled and shot, so what the hell do you do? What can you do? You just go forward because that's the only **bloke** you can take your knife in, that's the bloke you're facing.*

We were sent in to High Wood in broad daylight in the face of heavy machine-gun fire and shell fire, and everywhere there was dead bodies all over the place where previous battalions and regiments had taken part in their previous attacks. We went in there and C Company got a terrible bashing there. It was criminal to send men in broad daylight, into machine-gun fire, without any cover of any sort whatsoever. There was no need for it; they could have hung on and made an attack on the flanks somewhere or other, but we had to carry out our orders.

But there was one particular place just before we got to High Wood which was a crossroads, and it was really hell there, they shelled it like anything, you couldn't get past it, it was almost impossible. There were men everywhere, heaps of men, not one or two men, but heaps of men everywhere, all dead. Then afterwards, when our battle was all over, after our attack on High Wood, there was other battalions went up and they got the same! They went on and on.

Bloke: A British word for man.

They just seemed to be pushing men in to be killed and no reason. There didn't seem to be any reason. They couldn't possibly take the position, not on a frontal attack. Not at High Wood.

Most of the chaps, actually, they were afraid to go in because they knew it was death. Before we went in, we knew what would happen, some of the blokes that had survived from previous attacks knew what they'd been through. It was hell, it was impossible, utterly impossible. The only possible way to take High Wood was if the Germans ran short of ammunition, they might be able to take it then. They couldn't take it against machine-guns, just ridiculous. It was absolute slaughter. We always blamed the people up above. We had a saying in the Army, 'The higher, the fewer.' They meant the higher the rank, the fewer the brains. [Macdonald, pp. 160–61]

Excerpt from Good-bye to All That

Robert Graves
British army captain

[May 28th 1915]

Last night a lot of German stuff was flying about, including shrapnel. I heard one shell whish-whishing towards me and dropped flat. It burst just over the trench where 'Petticoat Lane' runs into 'Lowndes Square.' My ears sang as though there were gnats in them, and a bright scarlet light shone over everything. My shoulder got twisted in falling and I thought I had been hit, but I hadn't been. The vibration made my chest sing, too, in a curious way, and I lost my sense of equilibrium. I was ashamed when the sergeant-major came along the trench and found me on all fours, still unable to stand up straight. [Graves, p. 112]

Excerpt from 1914–1918: Voices and Images of the Great War

Sergeant Gottfried Kreibohm
German army, 10th Company, Lehr Infantry Regiment, 3rd Guard Division

[1916 — Battle of the Somme]

10 July. After being relieved in the morning we returned to the dug-out in the wood (High Wood). The artillery fire there was

'Petticoat Lane' runs into 'Lowndes Square': Soldiers named trenches after familiar streets. These trenches were named after streets in London, England.

absolutely frantic. Nearly every shell landed in the trench. Some men were buried alive while others were blown into the air. Unteroffizier Wahlen's squad had dug the deepest hole into the side of the trench for protection. It was too deep, for two shells landed directly on top of them and six men were entombed inside. We immediately began tearing away at the earth and could hear someone shouting, but our rescue efforts did not save everyone.

*11 July. At 4 a.m. I left with three men and took up residence in the field of craters between the company's forward trench and Mametz Wood. We immediately set to work deepening our holes, digging for two hours. Around eight o'clock the English began to systematically **strafe** the company sector with heavy-calibre shells. Geysers of earth a hundred feet high shot from the ground. With my field glasses I could see past Mametz Wood all the way to the village of Mametz. The entire area was swarming with the activity of English troops, wagons and ambulances moving forward, and prisoners going to the rear. It was a shame we did not have contact with our artillery. We sat watching this panorama until midday. No relief came. The shell fire increased in our vicinity and every fifteen minutes we had to shovel clods of earth from our holes. Pieces of equipment were sent flying out of the Company's trench while the barbed-wire stakes tumbled crazily in the air. The ground rumbled and heaved with each explosion. Suddenly, a noise like a roaring freight train rushed down upon me and I instinctively covered my head with my hands. I waited one, two, five agonising seconds—for the explosion. When nothing happened I opened my eyes and saw, to my immense relief, a large shell half buried in the earth only one and a half metres away from me. It was a dud. Thus we waited in our holes for ten hours—the most fearful ten hours I had ever experienced in my life.* [Macdonald, pp. 161–62]

Excerpt from Sagittarius Rising

Cecil Lewis

British Royal Flying Corps, Square pilot

[1916 – Battle of the Somme]

*Next morning I was allotted a machine and given my orders. . . . My flight-Commander was scandalized at my lack of experience. Twenty hours, the total my logbook showed, was no good to him. I was to take my **machine** and fly it all day. . . .*

Strafe: Attack with machine guns.

Machine: Airplane.

After ten hours of this came my first real job—to photograph the enemy second-line trenches. . . .

*If there was ever an aeroplane unsuited for active service it was the BE 2c. The pilot sat slightly **aft** of the main **planes** and had a fair view above and below, except where the lower main plane obscured the ground forward; but the observer, who sat in front of him, could see practically nothing, for he was wedged under the small center section, with a plane above, another below, and bracing wires all round. He carried a gun for defense purposes but he could not fire it forward, because of the propeller. Backwards, the center-section struts, wires, and the tail plane cramped his style. In all modern machines the positions are reversed; the pilot sits in front, leaving the observer a good field of fire aft and using his own guns, which can be fired through the propeller, forward. But in 1916 the synchronized gear enabling a machine gun to be fired through the whirling propeller and still miss the blades had not been perfected.*

The observer could not operate the camera from his seat because of the plane directly below him, so it was clamped on outside the fuselage, beside the pilot; a big, square, shiny mahogany box with a handle on top to change the plates (yes, plates!). To make an exposure you pulled a ring on the end of a cord. To sight it, you leaned over the side and looked through a ball and cross-wire finder. The pilot, then, had to fly the machine with his left hand, get over the spot on the ground he wanted to photograph—not so easy as you might think— put his arm out into the seventy-mile-an-hour wind, and push the camera handle back and forward to change the plates, pulling the string between each operation. Photography in 1916 was somewhat amateurish.

*So I set out on that sunny afternoon, with a sergeant-gunner in the front seat, and climbed up towards the lines. As I approached them, I made out the place where we were to start on the ground, comparing it with the map. Two miles the other side of the front line didn't look far on paper; but it seemed a devil of a way when you had to fly vertically over the spot. The sergeant knelt on his seat, placed a **drum** on the **Lewis gun**, and faced round over the tail, keeping a wary eye open for **Fokkers**. But the sky was deserted, the line quiet. **Jerry** was having a day off. I turned the machine round to start on my steady course above the trenches, when two little puffs of gray smoke appeared a hundred feet below us, on the left. The sergeant pointed and smiled: "**Archie!**" Then three others appeared closer, at our own height. It was funny the way the balls of smoke appeared magically*

Aft: Behind.

Planes: Wings.

Drum: A cartridge of ammunition.

Lewis Gun: A type of machine gun.

Fokkers: German planes.

Jerry: Slang for a German.

"Archie:" Antiaircraft weapons.

A German pilot stands in front of a Fokker DVII, one of Germany's best fighter planes. *(Archive Photos. Reproduced by permission.)*

Report: The sound of a firearm or explosive.

Range: Aim guns to hit a target.

in the empty air, and were followed a moment later by a little flat **report***. If they didn't* **range** *us any better than that they were not very formidable, I thought, and began to operate the camera handle.*

There are times in life when the faculties seem to be keyed up to superhuman tension. You are not necessarily doing anything; but you are in a state of awareness, of tremendous alertness, ready to act instantaneously should the need arise. Outwardly, that day, I was calm, busy keeping the trenches in the camera sight, manipulating the handle, pulling the string; but inside my heart was pounding and my nerves straining, waiting for something, I did not know what, to happen. It was my first job. I was under fire for the first time. Would Archie get the range? Would the dreaded Fokker appear? Would the engine give out? It was the fear of the unforeseen, the inescapable, the imminent hand of death which might, from moment to moment, be ruthlessly laid upon me. I realized, not then, but later, why pilots cracked up, why they lost their nerve and had to go home. Nobody could stand the strain indefinitely, ultimately it reduced you to a dithering state, near to imbecility. For always you had to fight it down, you had to go out and do the job, you could never admit it, never say frankly: "I am afraid. I can't face it any more." For cowardice, because, I suppose, it is the most common human emotion, is the most despised. And you did gain victories over yourself. You won and won and won again, and always there was another to be won on the morrow. They sent you home to rest, and you put it in the background of your mind; but it was not like a bodily fatigue from which you could completely recover, it was a sort of damage to the essential tissue of your being. You might have a greater willpower, greater stamina to fight down your failing; but a thoroughbred that has been lashed will rear at the sight of the whip, and never, once you had been through it, could you be quite the same again.

I went on pulling the string and changing the plates when, out of the corner of my eye, I saw something black ahead of the machine. I looked up quickly: there was nothing there. I blinked. Surely, if my eyes were worth anything, there had been something . . . Yes! There it was again! This time I focused. It was a howitzer shell, one of our own shells, slowing up as it reached the top of its trajectory, turning slowly over and over, like an ambling porpoise, and then plunging down to burst. Guns fire shells in a flat trajectory; howitzers fling them high, like a lobbed tennis ball. It follows that, if you happen to be at the right height, you catch the shell just as it hovers at its peak point. If you are quick-sighted you can then follow its course down to the ground. I watched the thing fascinated. Damn it, they weren't missing the machine by much, I thought; but I was left little time to consider it, for suddenly there was a sharp tearing sound like a close crack of thunder, and the machine was flung upwards by the force of the explosion of an Archie burst right underneath us. A split second later, and it would have been a direct hit. A long tear appeared in the fabric of the plane where a piece of shrapnel had gone through. There was a momentary smell of acrid smoke. "Ess! Ess!" shouted the sergeant. "They've ranged us!" I flung the machine over and flew west, then turned again, and again, and again. . . . The Archie bursts were distant now. We had thrown them off.

"How many more?" shouted the sergeant, with a jerk of his head to the camera box.

"Two."

Flying on a steady course is the surest way to get caught by Archie, and we had been, right enough. If we were quick we might snatch the other two photos and get away before he ranged us again. I turned back over the spot, pulled the string and flew on to make the last exposure, when the sergeant suddenly stiffened in his seat, cocked his gun, and pointed: "Fokker!"

As the war progressed, war planes—once used only for reconnaissance (information-gathering) missions—were being used to drop bombs over enemy territory. *(Archive Photos. Reproduced by permission.)*

I turned in my seat and saw the thin line of the monoplane coming down on our tail. He had seen the Archie bursts, no doubt, had a look round to see if we were escorted, and, finding it all clear, was coming down for a **sitter.**

I got the last photo as he opened fire. The distant chatter of his gun was hardly audible above the engine roar. It didn't seem to be directed at us. He was, I know now, an inexperienced pilot, he should have held his fire.

We replied with a chatter that deafened me, the **muzzle** of the Lewis gun right above my head. The Fokker hesitated, pulled over for a moment, and then turned at us again. The sergeant pulled his trigger. Nothing happened. "Jammed! jammed!" he shouted. He pulled frantically at the gun, while the stuttering Fokker came up. I put the old 2c right over to turn under him. As I did so, there was a sharp crack, and the little wind-screen a foot in front of my face showed a hole with a spider's web in the glass round it.

It was Triplex: no splinters; but another foot behind would have put that bullet through my head—which was not Triplex. A narrow shave. Instinctively I stood the machine on its head and dived for home. At that moment, as if to cap it all, the engine set up a fearful racket. The whole machine felt as if it would fall to pieces.

"Switch off! Switch off!" yelled the sergeant. "The engine's hit."

I obeyed, still diving, turning sharply as I did so to offer a more difficult target to the Fokker. But, luckily for us, he decided not to pursue. In those days the **Huns** did not adventure much beyond their own side of the line; and now we were back over ours.

We saw him zoom away again. He had us at his mercy, had he known. There was a moment of wonderful relief. We laughed. It had all happened in much less time than it takes to tell, and we were still alive, safe!

"Make for the advance landing-ground," shouted the sergeant. He was furious with the gun jamming, jumpy at our narrow shave, and, anyway, didn't relish his job with inexperienced pilots like me, just out from home. [Lewis, pp. 54, 55, 56–60]

Excerpt from *1914–1918: Voices and Images of the Great War*

Musketier Hans Otto Schetter

German army, 3rd Company, 231st Reserve Infanterie Regiment, 50th Reserve Division

[1917 — Third Battle of Ypres]

In the night of 19/20 September we **entrain** to the front line. Ledeghem, the last station open to traffic, is our unloading stop. Many ammunition columns pass by us toward the front, and the **cannonade** grows in intensity—giving us a welcome! The enemy is firing fiercely and our own artillery is replying in kind. This morning the

Sitter: A fight.

Muzzle: Barrel end of a firearm.

Huns: Slang for Germans.

Entrain: To travel by train.

Cannonade: Heavy artillery bombardment.

British infantry has broken through our first lines at Wilhelmstellung. Often we have to take cover on the side of the highway from the bursting shells. Anxiously I look ahead toward the front line where the shells are bursting with dark smoke clouds. Only stumps are left of the trees, and I try to figure out how I can best get through this hell. I am at watch at the roadside to look for vehicles of Regiment 231. We are moving forward with coffee containers and sacks of bread to our company which has occupied the shell holes and what is left of the trenches—the Flanders position. I am anxiously observing the battle-ground: concrete bunkers outline the position.

There are no quarters for us, so at night we sleep in a barn on top of potatoes. At 3 a.m. we are awakened and we now move forward in single file on the Menin-Ypres road. On both sides of the highway our **batteries** are firing and their iron greetings receive prompt reply from the enemy. We have to move fast because it is almost 6 a.m. and we have to reach our front line before daybreak. We reach the Front headquarters from where we are guided to our troops which occupy shell holes 150 metres ahead. The soldiers are reluctantly leaving their shell holes and are not eager for food. The whole earth is ploughed by the exploding shells and the holes are filled with water, and if you do not get killed by the shells you may drown in the craters. Broken wagons and dead horses are moved to the sides of the road; also, many dead soldiers are here. Seriously wounded who died in the ambulance wagon have been unloaded and their eyes stare at you. Sometimes an arm or a leg is missing. Everybody is rushing, running, trying to escape almost certain death in this hail of enemy shells on the highway, which is the only passage since the fields are flooded shell holes. I breathe easier when we reach our kitchen wagon. Today I have seen the real face of war. [Macdonald, pp. 242–43]

Excerpt from 1914–1918: Voices and Images of the Great War

Private J. Bowles

British army, 2nd/16th (County of London) Battalion, Queen's Westminster Rifles

[1917 – Battle of Messines]

We left the front line at 4 o'clock and it was nearly eight when we arrived at our dugouts, so you can guess how terrible the marching was through the trenches. After a week in the trenches this was supposed to be our rest. This is how we were treated.

Batteries: Army artillery units.

Wednesday. *Arrived dugouts 8 o'clock.*

Thursday. *Called us at 4.30 a.m. Marched us to* **RE dumping station,** *gave us planks to carry and marched us to the front line. Here we were split up into parties and sent down mines to carry sacks of earth up a long shaft and empty them on the* **parapet.** *It was the most terrible work I have ever been on, and we had to stick it for six hours, and then march all the way back. We were about dead when we got back, not only with the work, but with the march, for the trenches now are in an awful state. The rain continues every day, and in many places we were marching up to our knees in liquid mud. Of course, we worked all day in this state, and then had the same experience coming home.*

We arrived home at five in the evening, and the only food we had had was a bit of bread and cheese before starting. 'What can I do for England that does so much for me?' But we made a fire in our dugout, made some stew and were quite happy. I have mentioned mice and rats before but this place **licks creation!** *They go about in swarms and at night they are all over us. And they eat every mortal thing they can get at. We always carry an emergency ration in a bag in our pack. They got in our packs and ate the lot. They ate the pockets from the overcoats that covered us, the laces from my boots and the leather on our equipment, but no one has complained of being bitten. I shall not be sorry when we leave here, for rats in such numbers are abominable.*

To return to our work as miners. The day's work mentioned was repeated yesterday. Words fail me to describe it. Three men were compelled to fall out. A word about mines may be interesting. From a **sap** *that joins the firing line a tunnel is dug towards the German lines. In the one in which I was working, a stairway of some thirty rough steps at an angle of 45 degrees led to a chamber where there was an air pump and a* **windlass.** *From this chamber a tunnel ran right under the German lines, and down it was the railway with trucks pulled up by a wire on the windlass. It was our job to take the sacks from the trucks, carry them up the steps, take them about 100 yards along a trench and empty them. I was at this same mine yesterday, and at 10 o'clock we were all cleared out. An officer went down and with instruments heard Germans working and talking underneath. They had discovered our mine and were preparing to blow it up for us. What they will do about it I don't know but probably they will tunnel again and get under the Germans. What a game this is, and they call it war. It is not war, it is wholesale butchery, for in a mine they put up to 100 tons of* **ammonal**—*enough to blow a thousand men to pieces!*

RE dumping station: A storage place for supplies.

Parapet: A protective embankment for soldiers.

Licks creation: Tops all that he has seen before.

Sap: Covered trench.

Windlass: A hand-cranked or motor-driven machine used for lifting heavy objects.

Ammonal: Explosives.

Part of the night we were working on top, quite close to the German lines, with their machine-guns constantly spitting out death and their snipers having a shot when the star lights gave away our position. It is a case of working and ducking all the time until one feels inclined to say, 'Damn it all! Shoot me if you can.'

There was a brilliant moon one night and we worked in a more sheltered spot. Sitting on a sandbag on a beautiful night with machine-guns crackling and the large guns booming, one naturally thinks of home, only a hundred odd miles away and England peacefully slumbering, and your own bed empty waiting for you. 'Now then Sonny, get a move on,' and the picture vanishes and another load of sandbags must be emptied. [Macdonald, pp. 210–11]

Excerpt from Good-bye to All That

Robert Graves
British army captain

[Uncertain time frame]

*With the advance of summer came new types of bombs and trench-mortars, heavier shelling, improved gas-masks and a general tightening up of discipline. We met the first battalions of the New Army, and felt like scarecrows by comparison. Our Battalion went in and out of the Cambrin and Cuinchy trenches, with **billets** in Béthune and the neighbouring villages. By this time I had caught the pessimism of the First Division. Its spirit in the trenches was largely defensive; the idea being not to stir the Germans into more than their usual hostility. But casualties remained very heavy for trench warfare. Pessimism made everyone superstitious, and I found myself believing in signs of the most trivial nature.*

*Sergeant Smith, my second sergeant, told me of the officer who had commanded the platoon before I did. 'He was a nice gentleman, Sir, but very wild. Just before the Rue du Bois **show**, he says to me: "By the way, Sergeant, I'm going to get killed tomorrow. I know that. And I know that you're going to be all right. So see that my kit goes back to my people. You'll find their address in my pocket-book. You'll find five hundred francs there too. Now remember this, Sergeant Smith: you keep a hundred francs yourself and divide up the rest among the chaps left." He says: "Send my pocket-book back with my other stuff, Sergeant Smith, but for God's sake burn my*

Billets: Lodging for soldiers.

Show: A battle.

diary. They mustn't see that. I'm going to get it here!" He points to his forehead. And that's how it was. He got it through the forehead all right. I sent the stuff back to his parents. I divided up the money and I burned the diary.'

One day, walking along a trench at Cambrin, I suddenly dropped flat on my face; two seconds later a whiz-bang struck the back of the trench exactly where my head had been. The sergeant who was with me, walking a few steps ahead, turned round: 'Are you killed, Sir?' The shell was fired from a battery near Les Briques Farm, only a thousand yards away, so that I must have reacted almost simultaneously with the explosion of the gun. How did I know that the shell would be coming my way? [Graves, pp. 119–20]

Excerpt from The Storm of Steel: From the Diary of a German Storm-Troop Officer on the Western Front

Ernst Jünger

German officer

"Regniéville"

[July 1917] *Rations, too, were very poor. Beyond the thin mid-day soup, there was nothing but the third of a loaf, and something infinitesimal to eat with it, usually half-mouldy jam. Most of mine was always eaten by a fat rat, for which I often lay in wait, but in vain.*

This sparse living, which left us always half-fed, brought about a most unpleasant state of affairs. The men often suffered literally from hunger, and this led to pilfering of rations. . . . When it comes to food, the good manners that in Europe are mostly whitewash are soon scratched off. . . . Privations and danger tear away all that has been acquired, and then good form survives only in those in whom it is born. [Jünger, p. 192]

"The Great Offensive"

[1918]. . .*Everybody had that clutching feeling: 'It's coming over!' There was a terrific stupefying crash . . . the shell had burst in the midst of us. . . .*

I picked myself up half-conscious. The machine-gun ammunition in the large shell-hole, set alight by the explosion, was burning an intense pink glow. It illumined the rising fumes of the shell-burst,

Genocide in Armenia

An Excerpt from *Lines of Fire: Women Writers of World War I*, edited by Margaret R. Higonnet, 1999.

In January 1915 Turkish troops attacked Russian-held Kars in Armenia. The attack failed after only a few months, and the disappointed Turks began to suspect that Armenians living within Turkish borders had aided the Russians. Shortly after the failed offensive, the Turkish government began to deport and massacre Armenians living within the Turkish Empire.

As part of the deportation, in 1915 Gadarinée Dadourian and her five children were forced from their home in Gurun in eastern Anatolia. (Her husband was in America at the time.) In the following excerpt Dadourian recalls the **genocide**.

The deportation of Armenians from Gurun happened under the same conditions as everywhere else.

*The road we took to Der el Zor presented to view an enormous **hecatomb**. Luckily, my husband was already in America. I went into exile with my five children, three of whom died along the way, the two others at Der el Zor. . . .*

Once a week, groups of three to four thousand Armenians, under pretext of transporting them elsewhere, were taken away and exterminated. The river Murad was choked with corpses; an escort of military laborers was called to the spot to free the blocked waters of the river. The children of these martyrs were assembled in an orphanage; there were at least 6,000. Town criers warned that any Arab

in which there writhed a heap of black bodies and the shadowy forms of the survivors, who were rushing from the scene in all directions. At the same time rose a multitudinous tumult of pain and cries for help.

I will make no secret of it that after a moment's blank horror I took to my heels like the rest and ran aimlessly into the night. It was not till I had fallen head over heels into a small shell-hole that I understood what had happened. Only to hear and see no more! Only to get away, far away, and creep into a hole! And yet the other voice was heard: 'You are the company commander, man!' Exactly so. I do not say it in self-praise. . . . I have often observed in myself and others that an officer's sense of responsibility drowns his personal fears. There is a sticking-place, something to occupy the thoughts. So I forced myself back to the ghastly spot. . . .

Genocide: The systematic execution of a particular group, either national, racial, or political.

Hecatomb: A slaughter.

who sheltered Armenians in his house would be hung. They were authorized to keep only women, without children, as servants.

I was in the last caravan to leave the city; we knew they were leading us to our deaths. After two hours' march, we were halted at the foot of a hill. The Turks led the women in groups higher up. We did not know what was going on there. My turn came too; holding my two children by hand, I climbed the calvary [hill]. Horror! There was a well wide open where the executioners immediately threw the women they were stabbing. I received a sword blow on my head, another on my neck; my eyes were veiled at the moment I was thrown into the well with my children. I was on a pile of cadavers wet with blood. My head wound bled and my face was bloody.

I scarcely had the strength to drag myself toward a cavity in the well, where I lost consciousness. When I regained my senses I was in an Arab house. After the departure of the Turks, Arab women had come to search among the corpses in hope of finding some survivors. That is how they found me and seeing I was alive, they saved me. From then on I lived in this family as a servant.

I was anxious about the fate of my children, and the Arabs told me they had been taken in by other Arabs; I sought them but did not find them. Since orphans were carried to Constantinople, I went there in the hope of finding them. They must have died, because on the feast day of Bairam, the Turks took the thousands of children of Der el Zor outside the city, where they were burned alive. Only a few children survived by throwing themselves in the Euphrates [River], then gaining the further shore. [Higonnet, pp. 280–81]

The wounded men never ceased to utter their fearful cries. Some came creeping to me when they heard my voice and whimpered, 'Sir. . .Sir!' One of my favourite recruits, Jasinski, whose leg was broken by a splinter, caught hold of me round the knees. Cursing my impotence to help, I vainly clapped him on the shoulder. Such moments can never be forgotten.

I had to leave the wretched creatures to the one surviving stretcher bearer and lead the faithful few who remained and who collected round me away from the fatal spot. Half an hour before I had been at the head of a first-rate company at fighting strength. Now the few who followed me through the maze of trenches where I lost my way were utterly crestfallen. A young lad, a milksop, who a few days before had been jeered at by his companions because during training he had burst into tears over the weight of a box of ammuni-

tion, was now loyally hulking one along on our painful way after retrieving it from the scene of our disaster. When I saw that, I was finished. I threw myself on the ground and broke into convulsive sobs, while the men stood gloomily round me. [Jünger, pp. 245–46]

What happened next . . .

The fighting that everyone thought would only last for weeks dragged on for months, and then for years. The bloody stalemate along the Western Front caused the Allied forces and the Central Powers millions of casualties. The war also caused tremendous psychological stress—soldiers had never before been subject to such prolonged or bloody battles. The entrance of the American forces into battle in 1918 lifted the spirits of the suffering Allied soldiers along the front and became the turning point of the war.

Did you know . . .

- The wounded outnumbered the dead. According to the *World War One Sourcebook,* Russia had about 5 million wounded; France and Germany, 4.2 million each; Austria-Hungary, 3.6 million; Britain, 2 million; Italy, 950,000; and Turkey, 400,000.

- World War I caused a kind of psychological damage called shell shock, which had symptoms ranging from nervousness to mental collapse to complete paralysis.

- Shell shock in World War I is attributed to the unprecedented durations of enemy fire, long periods without sleep, and ongoing malnutrition. Soldiers of previous wars did not suffer from shell shock.

- The upper classes (those with social and educational advantages) suffered the heaviest casualties during the war because they were most often promoted to ranking officers. "In 1916, for example, the chances of an officer being killed were about double those of an 'other rank,'" according to the *World War One Sourcebook.*

For More Information

Books

Ellis, John. *Eye-Deep in Hell: Trench Warfare in World War I.* New York: Pantheon, 1976.

Graves, Robert. *Good-Bye to All That.* 2nd ed. New York: Anchor Books, Doubleday, 1957.

Haythornthwaite, Philip J. *The World War One Sourcebook.* London: Arms and Armour Press, 1992.

Higonnet, Margaret, ed. *Lines of Fire: Women Writers of World War I.* New York: Plume, 1999.

Jünger, Ernst. *The Storm of Steel: From the Diary of a German Storm-Troop Officer on the Western Front.* London: Chatto and Windus, 1929.

Lewis, Cecil. *Sagittarius Rising.* New York: Harcourt, Brace, and Company, 1936.

Macdonald, Lyn. *1914–1918: Voices and Images of the Great War.* London: Michael Joseph, 1988.

Rawling, Bill. *Surviving Trench Warfare: Technology and the Canadian Corps, 1914–1918.* Toronto: University of Toronto Press, 1992.

Web sites

The Great War and the Shaping of the 20th Century. [Online] http://www.pbs.org/greatwar (accessed October 2000).

Lycos Guide to Trench Warfare of World War I. [Online] http://www.lycos.com/wguide/wire/wire_17451773_93717_3_21.html (accessed March 2001).

The 1918 Influenza. [Online] http://www.library.utoronto.ca/spanishflu/1918.html (accessed December 2000).

World War I: Trenches on the Web. [Online] http://www.worldwar1.com (accessed October 2000).

Reactions to War's End from the Front

Excerpt from Lines of Fire: Women Writers of World War I

Edited by Margaret R. Higonnet. Translated by Trudi Nicholas from *Schwesterndienst im Weltkriege: Feldpostbriefe und Tagebuchblatter* Published in 1936

Excerpt from The Storm of Steel: From the Diary of a German Storm-Troop Officer on the Western Front

By Ernst Jünger Published in 1929

Excerpts from 1914–1918: Voices and Images of the Great War

Edited by Lyn Macdonald Published in 1988

World War I ended when the armistice was signed on November 11, 1918. The most tragic and devastating loss during the war was the loss of life. Millions of soldiers died in battle, and countless civilians were killed by the side effects of the war: starvation, disease, or—in the case of the Armenians in Turkey—genocide (see page 32). But the war also took something from the living: It snatched the youth of many men and women. In *Sagittarius Rising,* Cecil Lewis sums up an experience shared by many World War I soldiers: The war, Lewis remarks, "took me from school at sixteen, it destroyed all hope of University training or apprenticeship to a trade, it deprived me of the only carefree years, and washed me up, inequipped for any serious career, with a Military Cross, a Royal handshake, a six-hundred-pound gratuity, and—I almost forgot to say—my life." Speaking for all those who had only ever been trained to fight, Lewis continues, "[W]hen [the war] was over we had to start again."

Although some calculated that an entire generation was "lost" to the war, those who survived to put down their weapons on November 11 did return to lives of peace—for a

"I believe [history] will be completely unable to gauge the unspeakable suffering this war has brought. It will pass by without noticing those who became cripples in their prime. . .without noticing those thousands of women whose lives from now on are filled with loneliness. World history will roll on."

Kathe Russner German surgical sister, Red Cross

U.S. soldiers and citizens participating in one of the many peace celebrations held following the end of World War I. *(Archive Photos. Reproduced by permission.)*

while. The hundreds of thousands of soldiers who were on the front that November had different reactions to the end of the war. The following excerpts provide a glimpse of what it felt like to realize the end of the war. A German officer gains new appreciation for his fatherland; a German nurse laments the tremendous loss of life; a British soldier and his comrades are stunned; a French couple can only weep; a British prisoner of war walks freely again; and an American soldier celebrates.

Things to remember while reading the personal stories about the end of the war:

- Millions of people survived the war with terrible injuries. All told, the Allied forces had a casualty rate of about 52 percent—22 million of the 42 million men sent to war. The Central Powers lost 15 million of the 23 million men they mobilized, a 65 percent casualty rate. Austria-Hungary had the highest casualty rate—90 percent—followed by Russia at 76 percent and France at 73 percent.

- The armistice was signed on November 11, 1918. All fighting stopped on the Western Front.

- German troops left Belgium on November 26, 1918.

- On December 1, 1918, British and American troops entered German territories to begin the peacetime occupation.

- On June 28, 1919, the peace treaty was signed at Versailles, France.

Excerpt from Lines of Fire: Women Writers of World War I

Kathe Russner
German surgical sister, Red Cross, serving on the Western Front

Diary Pages and a Field Letter

October 9, 1918

*Today, Germany allegedly made a peace offer; it will surrender Belgium and Alsace-Lorraine. The **Alsatian** nurse who is now sharing a room with me and nurse J.G. wept bitterly at the thought of becoming French. J. and I ran to the railway station in hope of hearing some new reports. This uncertainty about the way things are brewing is almost unbearable. There were no new telegrams but we arrived just as a hospital train was being unloaded. A stretcher with a corpse was also laid on the platform. It lay there a long, long while before anyone had time to see to it. The living have priority! On the way back we picked up a few men with minor injuries who were walking around, searching for their assigned hospital. We showed them the way and took their heavy luggage from them. They looked pale and exhausted. When a railway official on the other side of the street saw our little troop, he came over and took the rest of their baggage.*

In the meantime the first admissions have arrived at our hospital. The room intended for the Reception is far too small. The great

Alsatian: An inhabitant of Alsace, a region between France, Germany, Belgium, and Switzerland.

entrance hall of the industrial school is already full: stretcher after stretcher crammed side by side. They wait to be deloused, bathed, and transferred to beds. Pale, haggard faces with hollow, feverish eyes. When they spot us, there are beseeching cries from all sides: "A drink, nurse, a drink!" We can barely fill the beakers and pass along the rows fast enough, so parched are their burning lips. And lots and lots of grateful looks and many a "thousand, thousand thanks" repay a little drop of water. . . .

October 11, 1918

My dear Father, I must write you a few lines, even though we have our hands completely full and I could drop with weariness. But I'd like to thank you for writing to me so regularly. Longingly I await your Sunday letters and would be bitterly disappointed if one did not arrive.

I can understand only too well how strongly you feel about the fate of our fatherland. It weighs on us too, like a ton. Only our charges, in their awful agony and in recollection of those horrors they left behind, which probably none of us can imagine, yearn for just one thing, peace, peace at home. Why, then, the sacrifice of all these lives? Thinking about it could drive one insane. Will posterity find an answer?

Posterity? I believe it will be completely unable to gauge the unspeakable suffering this war has brought. It will lead its own life, it will pass by without noticing those who became cripples in their prime, it will pass by without noticing those thousands of women whose lives from now on are filled with loneliness. World history will roll on.

And yet one thing we may not and must not forget: Germany is not yet a heap of rubble; German men and women must not yet work for the enemy. What that means we see here with our own eyes; or rather we can only suspect but cannot fathom it in all its harshness and tragedy. And that it has not yet come that far for us, we thank those who, in pain and agony, groan here that it is deplorable. Yesterday a parcel for our charges arrived from schoolgirls in Dresden, arranged through one of our nurses on leave. Little bags with five cigarettes or candies or the like, and most important, a charming little letter for each. For example, one wrote at the end, "You must not address me formally as 'Sie' when you write to me, because I am only eleven years old." You have no idea what joy this parcel brought. Not everyone by any means could receive something—every tenth man at best—but the little letters were passed around and faces brightened for a few hours. Indeed, it is truly startling how grateful the people are for the slightest relief from their lot, so grateful that one is ashamed. For what is it that we can do for them? Give them a little light and love and sunshine. What is that in comparison to what they have done for us, what they have surrendered in youth, strength, and future in order to protect us against the enemy? That we can never, never repay.

Is it not so, Father? And is it not terrible that there are so many now who have completely forgotten or else never fully grasped its magnitude? The poor fellows are immeasurably embittered by this. An **N.C.O.** from Baden, one of my charges, a profound and tender soul, tells me that people sometimes avoid soldiers on leave at home, or even mock them for 'shirking their duties,' etc. It is painful to hear and there are no words of comfort. I could only give him my hand— with tears in my eyes, I assure you—and say, "D., there are still those who know they have much to thank you for."

And now I have to ask you a huge favor. Recruit some friends and relatives for a collection of alms. If each contributes just a small trifle

N.C.O.: Noncommissioned officer, such as a sergeant or corporal.

A Soldier's Life: Reactions to War's End from the Front   41

and a kind word—a little can amount to a great deal! Tell them how bitterness gnaws at them all; how it makes them incapable of further sacrifice. Tell them how, even in feverish dreams, the thought of "Germany, home" pursues them; how responsive they are to an encouraging line from home. Tell them that, were it not for these fine, brave men, we would have a pile of rubble for a homeland and would have to serve the enemy.

Oh, if you were to see them here in their hundreds and thousands, young, once sturdy, merry fellows who now lie there as helpless as little children, who for weeks and months are unable to move one centimeter by themselves, for whom day after day, endless sleepless nights, week after week passes with grim and wretched thoughts about their future and that of their family. If you were to see them in their agony, if you heard the groans and lamentations that do not cease day or night, you would find the words to soften the coldest and most stubborn heart and to stir the indifferent. [Higonnet, pp. 225–27]

Excerpt from The Storm of Steel: From the Diary of a German Storm-Troop Officer on the Western Front

Ernst Jünger
German officer

. . . Why should I conceal that tears smarted in my eyes when I thought of the end of the enterprise in which I had borne my share? I had set out to the war gaily enough, thinking we were to hold a festival on which all the pride of youth was lavished, and I had thought little, once I was in the thick of it, about the ideal that I had to stand for. Now I looked back—four years of development in the midst of a generation predestined to death, spent in caves, smoke-filled trenches, and shell-illumined wastes; years enlivened only by the pleasures of a **mercenary**, and nights of guard after guard in an endless perspective; in short, a monotonous calendar full of hardships and privation, divided by the red-letter days of battles. And almost without any thought of mine, the idea of the Fatherland had been distilled from all these afflictions in a clearer and brighter essence. That was the final winnings in a game on which so often all had been staked: the nation was no longer for me an empty thought veiled in symbols; and how could it have been otherwise when I had seen so many die

Mercenary: Soldier.

for its sake, and been schooled myself to stake my life for its credit every minute, day and night, without a thought? And so, strange as it may sound, I learned from this very four years' schooling in force and in all the fantastic extravagance of material warfare that life has no depth of meaning except when it is pledged for an ideal, and that there are ideals in comparison with which the life of an individual and even of a people has no weight. And though the aim for which I fought as an individual, as an atom in the whole body of the army, was not to be achieved, though material force cast us, apparently, to the earth, yet we learned once and for all to stand for a cause and if necessary to fall as befitted men.

Hardened as scarcely another generation ever was in fire and flame, we could go into life as though from the anvil; into friendship, love, politics, professions, into all that destiny had in store. It is not every generation that is so favoured.

. . .Germany lives and Germany shall never go under! [Jünger, pp. 317–19]

Excerpt from 1914–1918: Voices and Images of the Great War

A. D. Pankhurst

British Corporal, 56th Division, Royal Field Artillery (Trench Mortars)

We were working towards Mons when the war finished, and moving about so we had trouble getting fed. On the night of 10 November we'd had no rations and our last food had been the midday meal of the day before, so I went off to try to find a source of supply. I walked for about an hour until I came to a small village where there was a chateau that was Divisional Headquarters and I went in and saw a staff officer and told him the position. He said, 'Right, I'll see to it.'

While I was waiting I saw a noticeboard nailed to a tree on a patch of grass outside the chateau and I struck a match to read it—for it was dark by now—and I read that an Armistice would be declared at 11 o'clock next day. This officer was as good as his word, because soon a **GS wagon** drove up, laden with food, and I got on it and off we went. We got back to the ammunition dump in the early hours of the morning and when they'd unloaded the food I roused the cook and said, 'I've got some food. Get up and make a meal.' He set to and made a bully beef stew, and when we sat down to our dinner

GS Wagon: A General Service military truck.

A crowd of soldiers on the Western Front celebrating as an officer announces the news of the armistice, November 11, 1918.
(Archive Photos. Reproduced by permission.)

Mafficking: Boisterous celebrating.

Blighty: Britain.

Bully beef: Corned or canned beef, an important source of protein for the British army.

it was breaking dawn. When we'd nearly finished the food I said to them casually, 'The war's over at 11 o'clock this morning.' Somebody said, 'Yeah?' Somebody else said, 'Go on!' They just went on eating! There was no jumping for joy or dancing around. We were so war weary that we were just ready to accept whatever came. When I read of the dancing in the fountains in Trafalgar Square and men riding on top of taxi-cabs going down the Strand and the **Mafficking** that went on in **Blighty**, my mind always goes back to us few men and the quiet way we took the news.

It was different in France. Near the dump there was an old couple in a small farm, and we'd been there to try and get something to eat and they didn't have a thing in the house—not a crumb! So later that morning I took them a share of our rations—a tin of milk, a tin of butter, a tin of **bully beef**, some bread, some tea. Someone had got hold of a copy of the Continental Daily Mail and on the front page was the announcement of the Armistice. I showed it to them and they just sat rocking back and forwards in their chairs with tears rolling down their faces. They'd been in occupied territory for practically the *whole of the war and they were virtually beaten, just resigned to whatever would happen to them. I shall always remember that old couple. They must have suffered so much, not to have shown some glimmer of happiness.* [Macdonald, p. 308]

Excerpt from 1914–1918: Voices and Images of the Great War

Tom Grady
American Sergeant, U.S. Army

11 November – Monday

Cold and raining. Runner in at 10.30 with order to cease firing at 11.00 a.m. Firing continued and we stood by. 306th Machine-Gun Company on my right lost twelve men at 10.55, when a high explosive landed in their position. At 11.00 sharp the shelling ceased on both sides and we don't know what to say. Captain came up and told us that the war was over. We were dumbfounded and finally came to and cheered—and it went down the line like wildfire. I reported Jones' death and marked his grave. Captain conducted a prayer and cried like a baby. Built a big fire and dried our clothes and the bully beef tasted like turkey. We told the new boys our tales and about the battles and they were heavy listeners. Other teams returned from outposts and we celebrated by burning captured ammunition and everything that would burn. [Macdonald, p. 313–14]

Excerpt from 1914–1918: Voices and Images of the Great War

C. M. Slack, MC

British Captain, 1st/4th Battalion, East Yorkshire Regiment (prisoner of war)

We eventually finished up in the barracks in Cologne, about three hundred of us, and not much food except what came in our parcels, and then the Armistice came along.

Then a few days after that they were still blowing the bugle for us to go out on parade—but we didn't. We said, 'No, we've won the war. We're not going to parade any more.' One day a fellow called Hicks, a Gunner Officer, said to me, 'Look here, Slack, we've won the war, will you walk round Cologne with me?' I said, 'Yes,' and we polished our buttons up and walked straight out past the sentry. Although we'd won the war the sentries were still there. We went out past the sentry. 'Halt!' 'It's all right, we're coming back.' We went on slowly, half expecting to get one in the back. We went into the cathedral and stayed there for about half an hour and nothing happened, no hue and cry, and we came out and crossed the Hohenzollern Bridge and back to the camp and that was that.

We'd seen some of the Germans coming back, the unconquered heroes, and they came back with their donkey carts and their goats and all sorts of things. A regular rabble, shouting and waving to the crowds who were cheering them on, banners across the road, 'Welcome home to our unconquered heroes!'

A day or two after that, four officers went down to the station with their suitcases and asked for four tickets for London and they were told, 'We're sorry, but the lines are broken,' and so they came back to the camp.

*Even though we were prisoners, we were paid. They gave us money and it had been debited against our account and it was accumulating all the time and there were three hundred of us. The senior officers went to the Cologne Authorities and said, 'Look here, can't we contact a boat?' so we chartered a boat down the Rhine. We stopped at Dusseldorf for the first night and some of the people put up at hotels. I put up at the equivalent of the YMCA, and about three in the morning a policeman was shaking my shoulder. 'Get back to the ship. They're rioting in the town.' Dusseldorf was a **red place** and they were going to burn all the hotels and places where these British officers were, so we got back into our ship, sailed on to Rotterdam, and there the British Authorities took us over. The next day they put us on their own boat and we landed in Hull, my old home town, a fortnight after the Armistice. We were the first people home. We came on our own. We just came!* [Macdonald, pp. 318–19]

What happened next . . .

In the aftermath of the war, the lives of the world's young men and women were destroyed and many people could not see what had been gained. Europe was in worse shape than it had been when the war began. Empires were

Red place: Slang for a Communist area.

shattered, governments fell, and violent and destructive regimes came to power in several of the combatant countries. Perhaps the only country to truly benefit from the war was the United States, which emerged as the world's greatest power. Almost every other country was drained nearly to destruction by the conflict. In the end, World War I settled nothing. It merely set the stage for a war that would surpass it in its measures of death and destruction—World War II.

Did you know . . .

- The Allies, who emerged victorious, saw 5,100,000 men die in battle or from wounds received in battle.

- The losing Central Powers lost 3,500,000 men.

- In *War and Social Change in the Twentieth Century*, historian Arthur Marwick estimates that the war produced 5 million widowed women, 9 million orphaned children, and 10 million refugees, people who fled from their homes because of the war.

For More Information

Books

Heyman, Neil M. *World War I.* Westport, CT: Greenwood Press, 1997.

Higonnet, Margaret, ed. *Lines of Fire: Women Writers of World War I.* New York: Plume, 1999.

Jünger, Ernst. *The Storm of Steel: From the Diary of a German Storm-Troop Officer on the Western Front.* London: Chatto and Windus, 1929.

Kirchberger, Joe H. *The First World War: An Eyewitness History.* New York: Facts on File, 1992.

Lewis, Cecil. *Sagittarius Rising.* New York: Harcourt, Brace, and Company, 1936.

Macdonald, Lyn. *1914–1918: Voices and Images of the Great War.* London: Michael Joseph, 1988.

Marwick, Arthur. *War and Social Change in the Twentieth Century: A Comparative Study of Britain, France, Germany, Russia and the United States.* New York: St. Martin's Press, 1974.

Stokesbury, James L. *A Short History of World War I.* New York: William Morrow, 1981.

Winter, Jay, and Blain Baggett. *The Great War and the Shaping of the 20th Century.* New York: Penguin Studio, 1996.

Web sites

Armistice. [Online] http://www.spartacus.schoolnet.co.uk/FWWarmistice. htm (accessed March 2001).

The Armistice Demands. [Online] http://www.lib.byu.edu/~rdh/wwi/1918/ armistice.html (accessed March 2001).

The Great War and the Shaping of the 20th Century. [Online] http://www. pbs.org/greatwar (accessed October 2000).

The 1918 Influenza. [Online] http://www.library.utoronto.ca/spanishflu/ 1918.html (accessed December 2000).

World War I: Trenches on the Web. [Online] http://www.worldwar1.com (accessed October 2000).

Documents of Diplomacy

2

W hen people think of war, they usually think of battles won and lost, of shooting and killing, of the glory of victory and the terror of defeat. But World War I, like all wars, was also a war of words. Leaders of the major European countries formed alliances with other countries in order to protect themselves from their enemies. These leaders and their diplomats—government officials who negotiated with officials from other countries—tried to present their positions clearly to other countries so that they might avoid war. And when war began, diplomats and generals used words to explain and justify the military action. Diplomats signed treaties, exchanged letters and notes, and issued ultimatums. These documents of diplomacy are essential to understanding how and why World War I took place.

Historians agree that the existence of treaties and alliances between the major European powers was one of the key reasons that World War I became such a large-scale conflict. In the late nineteenth century, Europe was composed of a number of countries with relatively equal levels of power. No single country was strong enough to dominate the continent, so each of the major countries made alliances, or formal friendships,

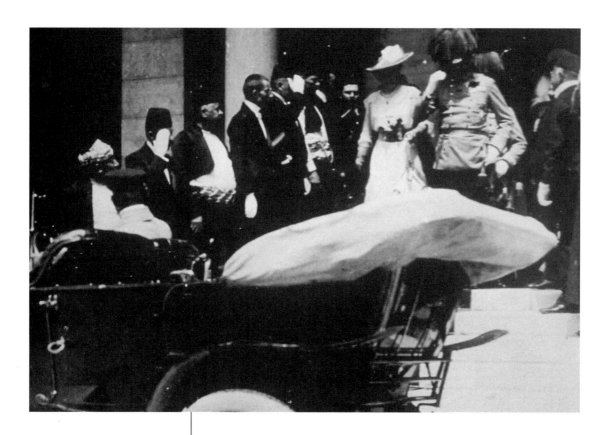

Archduke Franz Ferdinand and his wife, Countess Sophie, just moments before they were assassinated by a Serbian terrorist. *(Archive Photos. Reproduced by permission.)*

with other countries in order to gain strength. In 1879, Germany and Austria-Hungary pledged their friendship in what became known as the Dual Alliance. (Italy joined this alliance in 1882, making it the Triple Alliance, but withdrew once World War I began.) Germany, Austria-Hungary, and Italy promised to come to each other's aid if they were attacked by another country. In 1892, France and Russia signed a secret treaty that created bonds similar to those forged in the Dual Alliance. England signed a less formal agreement with France in 1904. From the moment those treaties were signed, a large-scale war became practically inevitable. If one country attacked another, all of Europe would be drawn into combat. That is exactly what happened in 1914. Archduke Franz Ferdinand (1863–1914), the heir to the Austrian throne, and his wife, Countess Sophie, were assassinated by a member of a Serbian terrorist group on June 28. Austria-Hungary threatened to attack Serbia; Russia came to the aid of Serbia; and by August every major European power found itself involved in the conflict.

The **Dual Alliance**—between the German Empire and the Austro-Hungarian empire—and the **Franco-Russian Alliance Military Convention** seemed to promise that each country would go to war to protect its ally. But this didn't mean that those countries wanted to go to war. In fact, leaders in Germany and Russia wanted very badly to avoid war. Germany's Kaiser Wilhelm II and Russia's Czar Nicholas II wrote a series of telegrams to each other in which they tried to think of any way they could avoid complying with the terms of the treaties that they had signed. The **Willy-Nicky Telegrams**, letters between blood relatives (the two were distant cousins), show a different side to European diplomacy.

By August 1, 1914, Germany, France, Russia, Austria-Hungary, and Serbia were all committed to war. But for Germany to enact its war plan—which called for an attack on France from the northeast—German troops had to cross neutral Belgium. The German ambassador to Belgium sent a confidential note to the Belgian foreign minister on August 2, 1914, asking for permission to cross Belgium. **The German Request for Free Passage through Belgium** and **Belgium's Response to the Request for Passage** offer insight into the ways countries justify their actions.

Secret Treaties

Dual Alliance

**Signed by the German Empire and the
Austro-Hungarian empire on October 7, 1879
Reprinted from the World War I
Document Archive, available online at
http://www.lib.byu.edu/~rdh/wwi/1914m/allyahg.html**

Franco-Russian Alliance Military Convention

**Signed by France and Russia on August 18, 1892
Reprinted from the World War I Document
Archive, available online at
http://www.lib.byu.edu/~rdh/wwi/1914m/franruss.html**

At the dawn of World War I western Europe looked much as it does today, with France and Germany the dominant geographic and economic powers on the continent. England, Russia, and the Austro-Hungarian empire were also important members of the European community. But Europe had only taken this political shape late in the nineteenth century. A scattering of independent Germanic states, under the leadership of the state of Prussia, had established dominance by defeating Denmark in 1863, Austria in 1865, and France in 1870. In January 1871 the Germans unified their twenty-six independent states into the German Empire and named Prussian King Wilhelm I (1797–1888) their emperor, or kaiser.

Germany was strong, but not strong enough to stand alone against the other countries of Europe, especially France, which longed to avenge its earlier defeat in the Franco-Prussian War (1870–71). Beginning in 1872, Germany sought to ally itself with Austria-Hungary, the aging empire to the south. By 1879 the two countries had signed a treaty called the Dual Alliance, which formally committed them to helping each other in the event of war. This treaty, reprinted below, made

> "Should, contrary to their hope, and against the loyal desire of [Germany and Austria-Hungary], one of the two Empires be attacked by Russia, the High Contracting Parties are bound to come to the assistance one of the other with the whole war strength of their Empires . . ."
>
> From the *Dual Alliance*

An 1890s political cartoon depicting the alliance between France and Russia. The powerful bear, symbolizing Russia, forces the French diplomat to "dance." *(Corbis Corporation. Reproduced by permission.)*

THE RUSSIAN-FRENCH ALLIANCE.

the alliance of Germany and Austria-Hungary the most dominant force in Europe—and a threat to other nations.

Though it had been defeated by Germany in 1871, France was still a proud and powerful nation. Following that defeat France expanded its military and built a strong economy. When Germany allied itself with Austria-Hungary, France also looked for an ally. It found that ally in Russia, the huge country that lies east of (western) Europe. Russia was ruled by an autocrat (one person who ruled with unlimited power) named Czar Nicholas II. Russia feared the growing influence of the Dual Alliance and especially wanted to limit that influence in Serbia and the rest of the Balkan states and provinces. In 1892 France and Russia joined in an alliance of their own, formalized in a document called the Franco-Russian Alliance Military Convention, reprinted below.

The documents reproduced below are translations of the actual secret treaties signed between Germany and Austria-

Hungary and between France and Russia. Secrecy was an important strength of both treaties. Because opposing countries did not have firsthand knowledge of the treaties, they did not know how the allied countries would act in a time of conflict. The secrecy of the documents probably only extended to their exact content, for opposing countries all knew of the friendship between the allied countries.

Things to remember while reading the treaties:

- These documents are written in diplomatic language which, like legal language, aims to be very precise so as not to allow for confusion. But it can be very difficult for nondiplomats to understand. As you read, try to put this diplomatic language into your own words to be sure that you understand what is meant.

- The Dual Alliance was renewed every five years until it was dissolved in 1918, along with the Austro-Hungarian empire.

- Article 2 of the Dual Alliance was especially written to allow the two allies to fight wars that did not involve the other ally. This article was designed to free Germany to wage war on France without Austro-Hungarian involvement, and to allow Austria-Hungary to settle issues in the Balkans without German intervention.

Dual Alliance between the German Empire and the Austro-Hungarian Empire

Signed October 7, 1879

*ARTICLE 1. Should, contrary to their hope, and against the loyal desire of the two **High Contracting Parties**, one of the two Empires be attacked by Russia, the High Contracting Parties are bound to come to the assistance one of the other with the whole war strength of their Empires, and accordingly only to conclude peace together and upon mutual agreement.*

High Contracting Parties: Germany and Austria-Hungary.

Not to support the aggressor: This meant that neither Germany nor Austria-Hungary would support any country that attacked its ally; this promise did not apply to Russia or countries supported by Russia, as the other clauses make clear.

Benevolent: Peaceful and assuming the best.

Stipulated: Determined by contract.

Reciprocal: Given to each other.

Becomes equally operative: Applies in this situation as well.

Provisionally fixed: Set, though the word "provisionally" means that it can be changed at the request of the contracting parties.

Emperor Alexander: Alexander II (1818–1881), the emperor of Russia from 1855 to 1881, who declared that Russia did not intend any attacks on Germany or Austria-Hungary when representatives from the three countries met at the Russian town of Alexandrovo.

Approbation: Approval.

Two Exalted Sovereigns: Kaiser Wilhelm of Germany and Emperor Franz Josef of Austria-Hungary.

Plenipotentiaries: Diplomatic representatives.

*ARTICLE 2. Should one of the High Contracting Parties be attacked by another Power, the other High Contracting Party binds itself hereby, not only **not to support the aggressor** against its high Ally, but to observe at least a **benevolent** neutral attitude towards its fellow Contracting Party.*

*Should, however, the attacking party in such a case be supported by Russia, either by an active cooperation or by military measures which constitute a menace to the Party attacked, then the obligation **stipulated** in Article 1 of this Treaty, for **reciprocal** assistance with the whole fighting force, **becomes equally operative,** and the conduct of the war by the two High Contracting Parties shall in this case also be in common until the conclusion of a common peace.*

*ARTICLE 3. The duration of this Treaty shall be **provisionally fixed** at five years from the day of ratification. One year before the expiration of this period the two High Contracting Parties shall consult together concerning the question whether the conditions serving as the basis of the Treaty still prevail, and reach an agreement in regard to the further continuance or possible modification of certain details. If in the course of the first month of the last year of the Treaty no invitation has been received from either side to open these negotiations, the Treaty shall be considered as renewed for a further period of three years.*

ARTICLE 4. This Treaty shall, in conformity with its peaceful character, and to avoid any misinterpretation, be kept secret by the two High Contracting Parties, and only communicated to a third Power upon a joint understanding between the two Parties, and according to the terms of a special Agreement.

*The two High Contracting Parties venture to hope, after the sentiments expressed by the **Emperor Alexander** at the meeting at Alexandrovo, that the armaments of Russia will not in reality prove to be menacing to them, and have on that account no reason for making a communication at present; should, however, this hope, contrary to their expectations, prove to be erroneous, the two High Contracting Parties would consider it their loyal obligation to let the Emperor Alexander know, at least confidentially, that they must consider an attack on either of them as directed against both.*

*ARTICLE 5. This Treaty shall derive its validity from the **approbation** of the **two Exalted Sovereigns** and shall be ratified within fourteen days after this approbation has been granted by Their Most Exalted Majesties. In witness whereof the **Plenipotentiaries** have signed this Treaty with their own hands and **affixed their arms.***

Done at Vienna, October 7, 1879

Franco-Russian Alliance Military Convention

Signed August 18, 1892

France and Russia, being **animated** by a common desire to preserve peace, and having no other object than to meet the necessities of a defensive war, provoked by an attack of the forces of the **Triple Alliance** against either of them, have agreed upon the following provisions:

1. If France is attacked by Germany, or by Italy supported by Germany, Russia shall employ all her available forces to attack Germany.

If Russia is attacked by Germany, or by Austria supported by Germany, France shall employ all her available forces to attack Germany.

2. In case the forces of the Triple Alliance, or of any one of the Powers belonging to it, should be **mobilized,** France and Russia, at the first news of this event and without previous agreement being necessary, shall mobilize immediately and simultaneously the whole of their forces, and shall transport them as far as possible to their **frontiers.**

3. The available forces to be employed against Germany shall be, on the part of France, 1,300,000 men, on the part of Russia, 700,000 or 800,000 men.

These forces shall engage to the full with such speed that Germany will have to fight simultaneously on the East and on the West.

4. The General Staffs of the Armies of the two countries shall cooperate with each other at all times in the preparation and facilitation of the execution of the measures mentioned above.

They shall communicate with each other, while there is still peace, all information relative to the armies of the Triple Alliance which is already in their possession or shall come into their possession.

Ways and means of corresponding in time of war shall be studied and worked out in advance.

5. France and Russia shall not conclude peace separately.

6. The present Convention shall have the same duration as the Triple Alliance.

7. All the clauses enumerated above shall be kept absolutely secret.

Affixed their arms: This probably means "joined their arms," similar to shaking hands to close a deal.

Animated: Motivated.

Triple Alliance: A revised version of the Dual Alliance that included Italy.

Mobilized: Brought into readiness for war.

Frontiers: Borders; in this case, the borders with their enemy.

No Separate Peace

The Dual Alliance and the Franco-Russian Alliance both contained important clauses that kept any of the parties that signed the treaties from declaring a "separate peace." These clauses meant that no nation could end the war without the agreement of its ally. When England decided to ally itself with France and Russia at the beginning of the war, the three countries issued an agreement proclaiming that none of them would negotiate for a separate peace. This document, signed on September 4, 1914, by diplomats from each of the countries, read as follows:

> The undersigned duly authorized thereto by their respective Governments hereby declare as follows: —
>
> The British, French, and Russian Governments mutually engage not to conclude peace separately during the present war. The three Governments agree that when terms of peace come to be discussed, no one of the Allies will demand terms of peace without the previous agreement of each of the other Allies.

(Reprinted from http://www.lib.byu.edu/~rdh/wwi/1914/ tripentente.html)

Unlike the Dual Alliance and the Franco-Russian Alliance, this agreement did not work out as planned. A revolution in Russia in 1917 removed the czar and his government from power, and the new revolutionary government did not feel compelled to obey the agreement. This new government negotiated a separate peace with Germany in 1918, which withdrew Russia from the war. By that time, however, the United States had come to the aid of France and England. If Russia had withdrawn its support earlier, or if the United States had not entered the war, World War I might well have ended very differently.

What happened next . . .

The Dual Alliance and the Franco-Russian Alliance worked as they were intended, by protecting their signers from having to fight a war alone. Yet these treaties were fatally flawed, for they turned what should have been only a minor skirmish between Austria-Hungary and Serbia into a major European war. After a Serbian-backed terrorist assassinated Austrian archduke Franz Ferdinand on June 28, 1914, Austria-Hungary decided to attack Serbia. Russia, Serbia's ally and protector, made it clear that it would come to Serbia's aid and fight Austria-Hungary. Once it appeared that Russia would fight Austria-Hungary, the other major European powers became involved. Austria-Hungary asked Germany for assistance under the terms of the Triple Alliance. Russia, seeing that it would be attacked by the Triple Alliance, asked France for help under the terms of the Franco-Russian Alliance. Soon England, which had signed its own secret alliance with France, also joined the war. The secret treaties worked, but at a terrible cost.

Did you know . . .

- The Dual Alliance agreement was revised and amended from its original version several times; it became the Triple Alliance in 1882 and was revised and renewed in 1912. The Franco-Russian Alliance of 1892 remained the same, but both France and Russia joined in separate agreements with England in 1904 and 1907, respectively. Despite these changes, the major provisions of both alliances were still in force at the start of World War I.

- One of the major goals of the Treaty of Versailles, the document that officially ended World War I, was to prohibit the signing of secret treaties. Opponents of secret treaties believed that countries would behave more carefully if they knew that their actions might create much bigger problems than they anticipated.

For More Information

Books

Clare, John D., ed. *First World War.* San Diego, CA: Harcourt Brace, 1995.

Kent, Zachary. *World War I: "The War to End Wars."* Hillside, NJ: Enslow, 1994.

Ross, Stewart. *Causes and Consequences of World War I.* Austin, TX: Raintree Steck-Vaughn, 1998.

Sommerville, Donald. *World War I: History of Warfare.* Austin, TX: Raintree Steck-Vaughn, 1999.

Stevenson, D. *The First World War and International Politics.* New York: Oxford University Press, 1988.

Stokesbury, James L. *A Short History of World War I.* New York: William Morrow, 1981.

Web sites

World War I Document Archive. [Online] http://www.lib.byu.edu/~rdh/wwi/ (accessed February 2001).

The Willy-Nicky Telegrams

Telegrams exchanged between Kaiser Wilhelm II (1859–1941) of Germany and Czar Nicholas II (1868–1918) of Russia

Reprinted from the World War I Document Archive, available online at http://www.lib.byu.edu/~rdh/wwi/1914/willynilly.html

In the closing days of July 1914, all of Europe shuddered at what appeared to be the unavoidable coming of war. Austria-Hungary seemed determined to attack Serbia, Russia seemed determined to defend Serbia, and everyone knew that once Austria-Hungary and Russia entered into war both Germany and France would follow. Military leaders in each of the European countries enacted plans to prepare for war: Soldiers were called for duty, ammunition was stockpiled, and trains were made ready. The newspapers brimmed with the latest war preparations. When Austria-Hungary declared war on Serbia on July 28, 1914, most people assumed that widespread war would soon follow. But at the centers of power, two men waged a last-ditch effort to prevent the larger war.

Kaiser Wilhelm II (1859–1941) of Germany and Czar Nicholas II (1868–1918) of Russia were the undisputed leaders of their countries. They each had nearly unlimited political power, and they each controlled the military forces of their respective countries. They also happened to be distant relatives; both were related to the former Russian empress Catherine the Great. Both men were willing to defend the honor of

"To try and avoid such a calamity as a European war I beg you in the name of our old friendship to do what you can to stop your allies from going too far."

"Nicky"

"With regard to the hearty and tender friendship which binds us . . . I am exerting my utmost influence to induce the Austrians to deal straightly to arrive to a satisfactory understanding with you."

"Willy"

In July 1914, Czar Nicholas II of Russia and Kaiser Wilhelm II of Germany (pictured here in 1910) attempted to prevent what soon developed into World War I. *(Corbis Corporation. Reproduced by permission.)*

their countries if war was required, but neither man believed that the fight between Austria-Hungary and Serbia was important enough to merit a larger war. So in the days leading up to the war, they opened a hurried personal correspondence aimed at putting a stop to the coming war. Their letters, excerpted below, are known as the Willy-Nicky telegrams, after the nicknames that the distant cousins had for one another.

Things to remember while reading the Willy-Nicky telegrams:

- Pay close attention to the date and time of the various telegrams, for these tell a great deal about the stress the two leaders were under. Some were sent very early in the morning. The first two telegrams, sent in the early-morning hours of July 29, actually crossed, as did the two messages sent on July 31.

The Austro-Hungarian Ultimatum to Serbia

When a Serbian-backed assassin killed Austrian archduke Franz Ferdinand—the nephew of Austrian emperor Franz Josef—and his wife on June 28, 1914, there was no doubt that Austria-Hungary would seek revenge. The question was, what form would that revenge take? Some in Austria wanted to investigate the killing like a normal criminal case. But more powerful people within Austria-Hungary—including the leader of Austria's armed forces—saw the murder as an opportunity to teach Serbia a lesson and gain more power in the Balkans (a group of countries occupying the Balkan Peninsula, including the Austro-Hungarian province of Bosnia and Herzegovina, as well as Serbia, Bulgaria, Romania, Greece, and parts of Turkey). Austria-Hungary saw a chance to gain territory by taking over parts of Serbia.

After nearly a month of debate, Austro-Hungarian diplomats issued an ultimatum (a list of demands that must be met to avoid attack) to Serbia on July 23, 1914. The Serbian government was asked to renounce (reject) all anti-Austrian propaganda, to arrest and punish any Serbian officials involved in the assassination, and to allow Austro-Hungarian officials to enter Serbia to oversee the investigation within Serbia. In their reply to the ultimatum, sent on July 25, 1914, the Serbs promised to aid in any criminal investigation; but they would not agree to let Austro-Hungarian officials enter Serbia, because they suspected that Austria-Hungary would use the opportunity as an excuse to send an occupying army. The Austro-Hungarians, who insisted that the Serbs accept the entire ultimatum, took the Serb response as a complete rejection of the ultimatum and decided to go to war. Against the urgings of Germany's Kaiser Wilhelm, Austria-Hungary declared war on Serbia on July 28, 1914.

- While Kaiser Wilhelm and Czar Nicholas were expressing to each other their desire for peace, they were also taking steps to prepare for war. Nicholas issued, withdrew, and reissued orders for Russian troops to mobilize; Wilhelm tried to convince Austria-Hungary to draw back from war, but he also prepared Germany's troops to fight on two fronts.

- Mobilizing armies was not the same as going to war, but it made war hard to avoid. Mobilization meant that soldiers reported for duty and prepared to follow their orders and go into battle. Once armies mobilized and military leaders took control of the armies' actions, it was difficult for political leaders to call the armies back.

- Austria-Hungary declared war on Serbia on July 28, 1914, and began shelling the Serbian capital the next day.

The Willy-Nicky Telegrams

July 29 to August 1, 1914

[Csar to Kaiser, July 29, 1:00 A.M.]

Peter's Court Palais, 29 July 1914
Sa Majesté l'Empereur
Neues Palais

*Am glad you are back. In this serious moment, I appeal to you to help me. An **ignoble** war has been declared to a weak country. The indignation in Russia shared fully by me is enormous. I foresee that very soon I shall be overwhelmed by the pressure forced upon me and be forced to take extreme measures which will lead to war. To try and avoid such a calamity as a European war I beg you in the name of our old friendship to do what you can to stop your allies from going too far.*

Nicky

[Kaiser to Csar, July 29, 1:45 A.M. This telegram crossed with the previous telegram.]

28 July 1914

*It is with the gravest concern that I hear of the impression which the action of Austria against Serbia is creating in your country. The **unscrupulous** agitation that has been going on in Serbia for years has resulted in the outrageous crime, to which Archduke Francis Ferdinand fell a victim. The spirit that led Serbians to murder their own king and his wife still dominates the country. You will doubtless agree with me that we both, you and me, have a common interest as well as all **Sovereigns** to insist that all the persons morally responsible for the dastardly murder should receive their deserved punishment. In this case politics plays no part at all.*

Sa Majesté l'Empereur: His Majesty the Emperor.

Neues Palais: The name of the czar's residence.

Ignoble: Not noble; common or lowly.

Unscrupulous: Dishonorable.

Sovereigns: Rulers.

On the other hand, I fully understand how difficult it is for you and your Government to face the drift of your public opinion. Therefore, with regard to the hearty and tender friendship which binds us both from long ago with firm ties, I am exerting my utmost influence to induce the Austrians to deal straightly to arrive to a satisfactory understanding with you. I confidently hope that you will help me in my efforts to smooth over difficulties that may still arise.@sph.txt:Your very sincere and devoted friend and cousin,

Willy

[Kaiser to Csar, July 29, 6:30 P.M.]

Berlin, 29 July 1914

I received your telegram and share your wish that peace should be maintained. But as I told you in my first telegram, I cannot consider Austria's action against **Servia** an "ignoble" war. Austria knows by experience that Servian promises on paper are wholly unreliable. I understand its action must be judged as trending to get full guarantee that the Servian promises shall become real facts. This my reasoning is borne out by the statement of the Austrian cabinet that Austria does not want to make any territorial conquests at the expense of Servia . I therefore suggest that it would be quite possible for Russia to remain a spectator of the [A]ustro-[S]ervian conflict without involving Europe in the most horrible war she ever witnessed. I think a direct understanding between your Government and Vienna possible and desirable, and as I already telegraphed to you, my Government is continuing its exercises to promote it. Of course military measures on the part of Russia would be looked upon by Austria as a calamity we both wish to avoid and jeopardize my position as mediator which I readily accepted on your appeal to my friendship and my help.

Willy

[Csar to Kaiser, July 29, 8:20 P.M.]

Peter's Court Palace, 29 July 1914

Thanks for your telegram **conciliatory** and friendly. Whereas official message presented today by your ambassador to my minister was conveyed in a very different tone. Beg you to explain this **divergency!** It would be right to give over the Austro-[S]ervian problem to the **Hague conference.** Trust in your wisdom and friendship.

Your loving Nicky

Servia: Serbia.

Conciliatory: Attempting to get along or to resolve past disputes.

Divergency: Difference between the ambassador's message and the kaiser's telegram.

Hague conference: An international court that ruled on disputes between countries.

[Kaiser to Csar, July 30, 1:20 A.M.]

Berlin, 30 July 1914

*Best thanks for telegram. It is quite out of the question that my ambassadors [sic] language could have been in contradiction with the **tenor** of my telegram. **Count Pourtalès** was instructed to draw the attention of your government to the danger & grave consequences involved by a mobilisation; I said the same in my telegram to you. Austria has only mobilised against Servia & only a part of her army. If, as it is now the case, according to the communication by you & your Government, Russia mobilises against Austria, my role as mediator you kindly intrusted [sic] me with, & which I accepted at you[r] **express prayer**, will be endangered if not ruined. The whole weight of the decision lies solely on you[r] shoulders now, who have to bear the responsibility for Peace or War.*

Willy

[Csar to Kaiser, July 30, 1:20 A.M.]

Peter's Court Palais, 30 July 1914

Thank you heartily for your quick answer. Am sending Tatischev [a diplomat] this evening with instructions. The military measures which have now come into force were decided five days ago for reasons of defence on account of Austria's preparations. I hope from all my heart that these measures won't in any way interfere with your part as mediator which I greatly value. We need your strong pressure on Austria to come to an understanding with us.

Nicky

[Kaiser to Csar, July 31]

Berlin, 31 July 1914

*On your appeal to my friendship and your call for assistance [I] began to mediate between your and the [A]ustro-[H]ungarian Government. While this action was proceeding your troops were mobilised against Austro-Hungary, my ally. Thereby, as I have already pointed out to you, my mediation has been made almost **illusory**.*

*I have nevertheless continued my action. I now receive authentic news of serious preparations for war on my Eastern frontier. Responsibility for the safety of my empire forces preventive measures of defence upon me. In my **endeavours** to maintain the peace of the world I have*

Tenor: Tone.

Count Pourtalès: The ambassador.

Express prayer: This is an elaborate way of saying "at your request."

Illusory: Like an illusion; he may mean unnecessary or pointless.

Endeavours: Efforts.

gone to the utmost limit possible. The responsibility for the disaster which is now threatening the whole civilized world will not be laid at my door. In this moment it still lies in your power to avert it. Nobody is threatening the honour or power of Russia who can well afford to await the result of my mediation. My friendship for you and your empire, transmitted to me by my grandfather on his deathbed has always been sacred to me and I have honestly often backed up Russia when she was in serious trouble especially in her last war.

The peace of Europe may still be maintained by you, if Russia will agree to stop the milit[ary] measures which must threaten Germany and Austro-Hungary.

Willy

[Csar to Kaiser, July 31. This telegram crossed with the previous telegram.]

Petersburg, Palace, 31 July 1914
Sa Majesté l'Empereur, Neues Palais

I thank you heartily for your mediation which begins to give one hope that all may yet end peacefully. It is technically impossible to stop our military preparations which were **obligatory** owing to Austria's mobilisation. We are far from wishing war. As long as the negociations [sic] with Austria on Servia's account are taking place my troops shall not make any **provocative action**. I give you my solemn word for this. I put all my trust in God's mercy and hope in your successful mediation in Vienna for the welfare of our countries and for the peace of Europe.

Your affectionate Nicky

[Kaiser to Csar, August 1]

Berlin, 1 August 1914

Thanks for your telegram. I yesterday pointed out to your government the way by which alone war may be avoided. Although I requested an answer for noon today, no telegram from my ambassador conveying an answer from your Government has reached me as yet. I therefore have been obliged to mobilise my army.

Immediate affirmative clear and unmistakable answer from your government is the only way to avoid endless misery. Until I have received this answer alas, I am unable to discuss the subject of your

Obligatory: Required; in this case, by treaty.

Provocative action: Warlike or decisive action, as opposed to mere preparations for war.

Czar Nicholas II of Russia, circa 1915. *(Archive Photos. Reproduced by permission.)*

telegram. As a matter of fact I must request you to immediatly [sic] order your troops on no account to commit the slightest act of trespassing over our frontiers.

Willy

[Csar to Kaiser, August 1]

Peter's Court, Palace, 1 August 1914
Sa Majesté l'Empereur
Berlin

I received your telegram. Understand you are obliged to mobilise but wish to have the same guarantee from you as I gave you, that these measures do not mean war and that we shall continue negociating [sic] for the benefit of our countries and universal peace deal to all our hearts. Our long proved friendship must succeed, with God's help, in avoiding bloodshed. Anxiously, full of confidence await your answer.

Nicky

What happened next . . .

Despite this flurry of telegrams, the two leaders were unable to stop the march to war. Germany felt compelled to honor its commitment to defend Austro-Hungary; Russia felt compelled to defend Serbia. On August 1, 1914, the day of Kaiser Wilhelm's final telegram to Czar Nicholas, Germany declared war on Russia. Other declarations of war followed like a line of dominoes once the first has been tipped: Germany declared war on France on August 3, England declared war on Germany on August 4, and Austria-Hungary declared war on Russia on August 6. Within a matter of days, battles were raging in Belgium, France, Germany, Russia, and Serbia. The disaster that Willy and Nicky had tried to avoid became a reality. For the next four years Europe and much of the world was plunged into the bloodiest and costliest conflict humans had ever witnessed.

Did you know . . .

- Though World War I started because of a conflict between Austria-Hungary and Serbia, few major battles took place in these two countries. Austria-Hungary and Germany invaded and eventually conquered Serbia by November 1915, and Serbia was not retaken until the end of the war.

- Kaiser Wilhelm II survived the war, but he was forced to abdicate (abandon) the throne of the German Empire in the weeks before the German surrender to the Allied forces on November 11, 1918. He spent the rest of his life in exile in Holland.

- Czar Nicholas abdicated the Russian throne on March 15, 1917, as his people rose up in revolution against his leadership. He and his family were held prisoner at a camp in the Russian town of Yekaterinburg, where they were all assassinated in 1918.

For More Information

Books

Clare, John D., ed. *First World War.* San Diego, CA: Harcourt Brace, 1995.

Kent, Zachary. *World War I: "The War to End Wars."* Hillside, NJ: Enslow, 1994.

Levine, Isaac Don, ed. *The Kaiser's Letters to the Tsar, Copied from the Government Archives in Petrograd, and brought from Russia.* London: Hodder and Stoughton, Ltd, 1920.

Ross, Stewart. *Causes and Consequences of World War I.* Austin, TX: Raintree Steck-Vaughn, 1998.

Sommerville, Donald. *World War I: History of Warfare.* Austin, TX: Raintree Steck-Vaughn, 1999.

Stevenson, D. *The First World War and International Politics.* New York: Oxford University Press, 1988.

Stokesbury, James L. *A Short History of World War I.* New York: William Morrow, 1981.

Web sites

World War I Document Archive. [Online] http://www.lib.byu.edu/~rdh/wwi/1914/willynilly.html (accessed February 2001).

Germany's Passage through Belgium

The German Request for Free Passage through Belgium

Reprinted from the World War I Document Archive, available online at http://www.lib.byu.edu/~rdh/ wwi/1914/germpassbelg.html

Belgium's Response to the Request for Passage

Reprinted from the World War I Document Archive, available online at http://www.lib.byu.edu/~rdh/ wwi/1914/belgsayno.html

A s soon as Germany decided to go to war against Russia and France, it set into motion war plans that had been prepared well in advance. The German war plan was known as the Schlieffen plan, named after Count Alfred von Schlieffen (1833–1913), who was chief of the German general staff from 1891 to 1905. Schlieffen predicted that Germany would one day be involved in a two-front war against France and Russia (a front is an area of contact between opposing forces in battle). The Schlieffen plan offered a way for the Germans to win such a war by first defeating the French and then turning their attention to the Russians.

In the first stage of the Schlieffen plan, Germany hoped to draw the French forces into the Alsace-Lorraine region of Germany (the region had once belonged to France). As the French committed themselves to battle in this region, the main German force would cross Luxembourg and Belgium and begin entering France all along its northeastern border. By sweeping southward and westward, the Germans would then quickly capture Paris (the capital of France), cut off French supply lines, and encircle the entire French army.

> "If this hope is disappointed, the Belgian Government are firmly resolved to repel, by all the means in their power, every attack upon their rights."
>
> *From Belgium's Response to the Request for Passage*

German army officers post a decree of war on August 1, 1914. *(Corbis Corporation. Reproduced by permission.)*

Once they had defeated the French army, the Germans would speed back across Germany on its well-developed rail system and defeat the Russians, who might not yet be organized enough to do battle.

There was one problem with the Schlieffen plan: It required that Germany first cross Belgium, a neutral country that wanted no part of a major European war. Germany could not simply invade and conquer Belgium without creating negative feelings in other countries. More importantly, Germany did not want England to become involved in the war; yet the Germans knew that England would not stand by and do nothing if Germany invaded Belgium. International law required combatants to respect the rights of neutral countries. In order to create the appearance that they were behaving in accordance with the law, German diplomats made a formal request to enter Belgium. That request, reprinted below, was delivered to Belgian minister for foreign affairs M. Davignon by the German ambassador at Brussels, Herr von Below Saleske, on August 2, 1914. Davignon delivered Belgium's reply, also reprinted below, on the following day.

Things to remember while reading the exchange between German and Belgian diplomats regarding German entry into Belgium:

- Germany's note to Belgium is an excellent example of how diplomatic language can be used to disguise an unprovoked attack. Germany knew very well that Belgium had to refuse the request to open the country's borders to a conquering army.

- Germany invented the story of a planned French invasion in order to give the Belgians a face-saving reason to accept Germany's invasion. Historians know of no plans on the part of France to invade Belgium. Does knowing this change the way you read the German request?

- Belgian diplomats, who knew very well what Germany was up to, wisely pointed out that Germany was about to take actions that were morally wrong and illegal.

- By August 2, the day the German note was delivered to Belgium, German troops were already lined up along Belgium's border.

German soldiers crossing the Belgian countryside in **August 1914.** *(Archive Photos. Reproduced by permission.)*

The German Request for Free Passage through Belgium

August 2, 1914

(Very Confidential)

RELIABLE information has been received by the German Government to the effect that French forces intend to march on the line of the Meuse [River] by Givet and Namur. This information leaves no doubt as to the intention of France to march through Belgian territory against Germany.

The German Government cannot but fear that Belgium, in spite of the utmost goodwill, will be unable, without assistance, to repel so considerable a French invasion with sufficient prospect of success to afford an adequate guarantee against danger to Germany. It is essential for the self-defence of Germany that she should anticipate any such hostile attack. The German Government would, however, feel the deepest regret if Belgium regarded as an act of hostility against herself the fact that the measures of Germany's opponents force Germany, for her own protection, to enter Belgian territory.

In order to exclude any possibility of misunderstanding, the German Government make the following declaration: —

1. Germany has in view no act of hostility against Belgium. In the event of Belgium being prepared in the coming war to maintain an attitude of friendly neutrality towards Germany, **the German Government bind them selves, at the conclusion of peace, to guarantee the possessions and independence of the Belgian Kingdom in full.**

2. Germany undertakes, under the above-mentioned condition, to evacuate Belgian territory on the conclusion of peace.

3. If Belgium adopts a friendly attitude, Germany is prepared, in cooperation with the Belgian authorities, **to purchase all necessaries for her troops against a cash payment, and to pay an indemnity for any damage that may have been caused by German troops.**

4. Should Belgium oppose the German troops, and in particular should she throw difficulties in the way of their march by a resistance of the fortresses on the Meuse, or by destroying railways, roads, tunnels, or other similar works, Germany will, to her regret, be compelled to consider Belgium as an enemy.

In this event, Germany can undertake no obligations towards Belgium, but the eventual adjustment of the relations between the two States must be left to the **decision of arms.**

The German Government, however, entertain the distinct hope that this eventuality will not occur, and that the Belgian Government will know how to take the necessary measures to prevent the occurrence of incidents such as those mentioned. In this case the friendly ties which bind the two neighbouring States will grow stronger and more enduring.

Belgium's Response to the Request for Passage

3 August, 1914

. . .This note [asking free passage] has made a deep and painful impression upon the Belgian Government. The intentions attributed to France by Germany are in contradiction to the formal declarations

The German Government bind them selves . . . to guarantee the possessions and independence of the Belgian Kingdom in full: Germany is saying that, as long as Belgium acts in a friendly manner toward Germany, Germany promises to make up for any Belgian property destroyed by Germany and respect Belgium's independence after the war. That is, Germany's occupation of Belgian territory would only be temporary.

To purchase all necessaries for her troops . . . and to pay an indemnity for any damage that may have been caused by German troops: Germany is offering to pay cash for any supplies it needs for its troops and to pay in advance for any damage those troops may cause.

Decision of arms: This means that the winner(s) of the war will determine relations between Germany and Belgium.

*made to us on August 1, in the name of the French Government. Moreover, if, contrary to our expectation, Belgian neutrality should be violated by France, Belgium intends to fulfil her international obligations and the Belgian army would offer the most vigorous resistance to the invader. The **treaties of 1839, confirmed by the treaties of 1870,** vouch for the independence and neutrality of Belgium under the guarantee of the **Powers,** and notably of the Government of **His Majesty the King** of Prussia.*

Belgium has always been faithful to her international obligations, she has carried out her duties in a spirit of loyal impartiality, and she has left nothing undone to maintain and enforce respect for her neutrality.

*The attack upon her independence with which the German Government threaten her constitutes a **flagrant** violation of international law. No strategic interest justifies such a violation of law.*

The Belgian Government, if they were to accept the proposals submitted to them, would sacrifice the honour of the nation and betray their duty towards Europe.

Conscious of the part which Belgium has played for more than eighty years in the civilisation of the world, they refuse to believe that the independence of Belgium can only be preserved at the price of the violation of her neutrality.

If this hope is disappointed, the Belgian Government are firmly resolved to repel, by all the means in their power, every attack upon their rights.

Treaties of 1839 . . . treaties of 1870: These treaties between European powers guaranteed the independence of Belgium, which had been created in 1831.

Powers: The leading powers of Europe: France, Germany, England, and Austria-Hungary.

His Majesty the King of Prussia. The formal title of Germany's Kaiser Wilhelm II.

Flagrant: Open and blatant.

What happened next . . .

Germany declared war on Belgium on August 4 and almost simultaneously attacked the Belgian fortress town of Liège. The Belgian army, commanded by King Albert I (1875–1934), was willing to fight, but they had never planned to counter an army as strong as Germany's. From a string of solidly built forts surrounding Liège, the Belgians fought off the German army for over a week. After August 12, however, the Germans overran the forts and pushed deeper into the country. The Germans moved quickly across Belgium, facing scattered resistance from the Belgian army. By the end of the

third week in August, German forces were approaching the French border and preparing to invade France.

The German attack on Belgium had convinced England that she must join with France and Russia to repel the **Central Powers.** England declared war on Germany on the very day that Germany entered Belgium, and British forces proved essential to slowing and finally stopping the advance of the German armies in the fall of 1914. By October 1914, German and Allied forces had deadlocked in a long line of trenches that ran across France and Belgium (this area was called the Western Front). Both sides committed themselves to winning a war that would soon come to seem unwinnable.

Did you know . . .

- When World War I began, most countries believed that it would be a short war, fought in a few decisive battles and decided by the fall of 1914. But modern weaponry and improved defensive tactics—especially trench warfare—

German soldiers attempting to sleep in their trench along the Western Front as two others stand guard. *(Archive Photos. Reproduced by permission.)*

Central Powers: The alliance of Germany and Austro-Hungary, which later grew to include the Ottoman Empire and several other countries.

turned the war into a battle of endurance that lasted over four years.

- Belgium had a tiny and poorly armed army. With just 117,000 men in uniform, the Belgian army was no match for Germany's 4,500,000 troops.

For More Information

Books

Clare, John D., ed. *First World War*. San Diego, CA: Harcourt Brace, 1995.

Kent, Zachary. *World War I: "The War to End Wars."* Hillside, NJ: Enslow, 1994.

Ross, Stewart. *Causes and Consequences of World War I*. Austin, TX: Raintree Steck-Vaughn, 1998.

Sommerville, Donald. *World War I: History of Warfare*. Austin, TX: Raintree Steck-Vaughn, 1999.

Stevenson, D. *The First World War and International Politics*. New York: Oxford University Press, 1988.

Stokesbury, James L. *A Short History of World War I*. New York: William Morrow, 1981.

Web sites

World War I Document Archive. [Online] http://www.lib.byu.edu/~rdh/wwi/ (accessed February 2001).

America's Emergence As A World Power

3

The United States experienced far less loss of life than its allies in World War I, and none of the physical devastation that was visited upon France, Italy, Belgium, and several other Allied countries. Nevertheless, the United States was profoundly changed by its involvement in World War I. When the war started in August 1914, the U.S. government was strongly committed to neutrality (not taking sides) and thought that it could avoid the problems of a European war. As the war progressed, however, it became obvious that neutrality was no longer possible. American ships were regularly sunk by German submarines, and France and Great Britain, longtime friends of America, implored the United States to enter the war. Finally, in 1917, America ended its policy of neutrality and joined the Allies (led by France, Great Britain, Belgium, and Italy) in their fight against the Central Powers (Germany and Austria-Hungary).

The U.S.'s decision to declare war on Germany on April 6, 1917, ended something besides three years of neutrality: It marked an important shift in American foreign policy. Ever since America was founded, it had prided itself on keeping its distance from the diplomatic policies of European nations; policies which U.S. leaders believed to be corrupt. The United States, its leaders declared, would represent the interests of the people and would not engage in the imperialism (the policy of extending a nation's power by aggressively acquiring territory) and secret treaties favored by **autocratic** European leaders. Thus for hundreds of years the United States pursued a policy that has been termed "isolationism," steadfastly avoiding entanglement in European problems.

By the turn of the twentieth century, however, it had become increasingly difficult for the United States to maintain isolation from world affairs. The American economy grew rapidly in the nineteenth century, and American businessmen looked for foreign markets for their goods. By the time World War I started, Americans were thoroughly engaged in foreign trade and depended on nations throughout the world for the exchange of goods. Could the United States remain a neutral trading partner of European countries who were engaged in a bloody war with each other? In truth, it could not.

Although American merchants provided supplies to both Allied and Central Powers at the beginning of the war, the North Sea blockade that England enforced against Germany quickly made trade difficult with the Central Powers. American merchants soon were providing goods mostly to Allied countries, especially England. Germany wanted such trade to stop, for it knew that a well-supplied England was a strong England. To disrupt trade between America and England, German submarines sometimes stopped American ships and seized goods. Such polite and bloodless seizures did not stop American merchants from trading and Germany soon made more aggressive attacks on American merchant ships. German submarines began attacking and sinking American and other neutral vessels, killing those aboard. Trading with mainly Allied nations had broken the bonds of neutrality in Germany's opinion, and Germany treated American merchants as opponents in the war. To protect its economic interests and the lives of its citizens, the United States would have to engage in warfare.

The decision to enter the war alongside the Allies was not an easy one. There was a deep belief among many American citizens and politicians that the United States should stay

Autocratic: Unlimited power.

out of the war. President Woodrow Wilson (1856–1924) originally shared this firm belief in U.S. neutrality, but eventually
he came to believe that America must fight in order to put an
end to the terrible war and lay the plans for peaceful interac-
tions between countries after the war. He called for the
entrance of the United States into the war not just to protect
American lives but to make the world "safe for democracy."

The documents excerpted in this chapter show the
slow development of the official American policies regarding
the war. The first document, **Declaration of Neutrality**, is
from a speech given by President Wilson to the Senate just
after the start of the war. In this speech Wilson asks Americans
to stay neutral "in fact as well as in name" (which meant to
speak and act in impartial ways toward the Central Powers and
the Allies) so that they may act as impartial (fair) mediators in
the war. The second document is Woodrow Wilson's **War Message**, issued on April 2, 1917. In this message, Wilson explains
to Congress why the United States can no longer remain neu-

U.S. president Woodrow
Wilson fought to keep the
nation neutral in the face of
World War I. He eventually
called for the entrance of
the U. S. into the war not
just to protect American
lives but to make the world
"safe for democracy."
*(Archive Photos. Reproduced
by permission.)*

tral. The final document is arguably the single most important diplomatic document of the entire war; it is known as **Woodrow Wilson's Fourteen Points.** In this address, given before Congress on January 8, 1918, Wilson proposes ground rules for establishing peace between the Allies and the Central Powers. The Fourteen Points became the basis on which the Allies eventually negotiated the Treaty of Versailles—the agreement that officially ended World War I. Wilson's Fourteen Points speech is also important because it shows Wilson pushing America to venture even further in its engagement with international politics. Wilson wanted the United States to lead an international rule-making body called the League of Nations. Though Wilson's isolationist opponents in Congress kept the United States from joining the League of Nations, Wilson's idea that America should become more involved in world affairs became the dominant force in U.S. foreign policy following World War II (1939–45).

Woodrow Wilson's Declaration of Neutrality

Delivered before the U.S. Senate
on August 19, 1914

Reprinted from the World War I Document Archive,
available online at http://www.lib.byu.edu/
~rdh/wwi/1914/wilsonneut.html

In early August 1914, the nations of Europe took up arms against one another in a war that came to be known as World War I. While tensions in Europe had been growing for many years, the armed conflict was triggered by a single event that occurred in a distant corner of the Austro-Hungarian empire. On June 28, 1914, Serbian-backed terrorists assassinated the crown prince of Austria in the provincial town of Sarajevo. Austria-Hungary and Serbia prepared to go to war. But treaty obligations between the major European powers soon made matters much worse: Germany promised its support to Austria-Hungary; Russia backed Serbia; and France backed Russia. What should have been a small war in the Balkans soon turned into a big war between the major European powers.

Americans watched the events unfolding in Europe with horror. They could not comprehend why so many people would rush into war for so little reason. Most Americans were quite happy that their country had a long tradition of avoiding European conflicts. They did not want to waste American lives on a war most considered pointless, and they did not want to disrupt their economy just to preserve a treaty. But

"The United States must be neutral in fact, as well as in name, during these days that are to try men's souls."

Woodrow Wilson

A 1916 Nelson Harding political cartoon depicts Woodrow Wilson's efforts to keep the U.S. out of World War I. President Wilson swinging the bat of "demand" misses the ball of "evasion" pitched by Kaiser Wilhelm II of Germany. *(Archive Photos. Reproduced by permission.)*

"PUTTING ONE OVER"

Americans also had strong ties to Europe. Many of them had parents or grandparents who had come from European countries, and many Americans still had close relatives living in Europe. Immigrants and descendants of immigrants from the various warring countries could not help but feel sympathy for "their" side. How would America handle itself in the face of these conflicting emotions? President Woodrow Wilson offered a plan.

Wilson knew that many Americans felt strongly about the war. After all, one-third of the American population was either foreign-born or had parents living in a foreign country. But Wilson had a vision of how the United States should behave during the war. He believed that if the United States could act impartially, not favoring one side or the other, it could actually benefit from the war. It could keep its economy strong by providing the European countries with food and supplies, and when the warring countries had had enough fighting, the United States could play the role of peacekeeper. Wilson spelled out this vision for the American people in a message he gave before Congress on August 19, 1914, just over two weeks after the war had started.

Things to remember while reading President Wilson's Declaration of Neutrality:

- Presidential addresses before Congress are important documents of foreign policy. Such speeches announce the goals and programs of the government. Wilson's speech was not only read by ordinary American citizens in their daily newspapers, but also by the leaders of powerful foreign nations.

- In 1914, when President Wilson gave this speech, there were no televisions or radios. Americans learned of presidential speeches in their newspapers, which were much more widely read than they are today.

- One of President Wilson's main concerns was that Americans might fight among themselves over European politics. He knew that there were large communities of Americans with family roots in Germany, France, England, and other combatant countries. He wanted to make sure that these Americans would put aside their European loyalties and conform to a single American approach to the war.

- Woodrow Wilson was well known as an orator, a skilled and eloquent public speaker. His speeches were carefully designed to persuade people to share his opinion, and they consisted of carefully constructed arguments. Note how Wilson uses certain techniques to emphasize his points, such as pairing similar words or using dramatic phrases in key sections of his speeches. Because Wilson was highly educated, he also used a variety of difficult and even old-fashioned words.

Declaration of Neutrality

My fellow countrymen: I suppose that every thoughtful man in America has asked himself, during these last troubled weeks, what influence the European war may exert upon the United States. . . .

The effect of the war upon the United States will depend upon what American citizens say and do. Every man who really loves America will act and speak in the true spirit of neutrality, which is the spirit of impartiality and fairness and friendliness to all concerned. The spirit of the Nation in this critical matter will be determined largely by what individuals and society and those gathered in public meetings do and say, upon what newspapers and magazines contain, upon what ministers utter in their pulpits, and men proclaim as their opinions on the street.

*The people of the United States are drawn from many nations, and chiefly from the nations now at war. It is natural and inevitable that there should be the utmost variety of sympathy and desire among them with regard to the issues and circumstances of the conflict. Some will wish one nation, others another, to succeed in the momentous struggle. It will be easy to excite passion and difficult to **allay** it. Those responsible for exciting it will assume a heavy responsibility, responsibility for no less a thing than that the people of the United States . . . may be divided in camps of hostile opinion, hot against each other, involved in the war itself in impulse and opinion if not in action.*

*Such divisions amongst us would be fatal to our peace of mind and might seriously stand in the way of the proper performance of our duty as the one great nation at peace, the one people holding itself ready to play a part of impartial mediation and **speak the counsels of peace and accommodation**, not as a **partisan**, but as a friend.*

I venture, therefore, my fellow countrymen, to speak a solemn word of warning to you against that deepest, most subtle, most essential breach of neutrality which may spring out of partisanship, out of passionately taking sides. The United States must be neutral in fact, as well as in name, during these days that are to try men's souls. We must be impartial in thought as well as in action, must put a curb upon our sentiments as well as upon every transaction that might be construed as a preference of one party to the struggle before another.

Allay: Calm, or relieve the intensity of.

Speak the counsels of peace and accommodation: Wilson is offering to defend the cause of peace and reason when others can speak only of war.

Partisan: Strong supporter of one side of an argument or dispute.

My thought is of America. I am speaking, I feel sure, the earnest wish and purpose of every thoughtful American that this great country of ours [. . .] should show herself in this time of peculiar trial a Nation fit beyond others to exhibit the fine poise of undisturbed judgment, the dignity of self-control, the efficiency of dispassionate action; a Nation that neither sits in judgment upon others nor is disturbed in her own counsels and which keeps herself fit and free to do what is honest and disinterested and truly serviceable for the peace of the world. . . .

What happened next . . .

America did stay officially neutral for nearly two and a half years, but it was not easy. From the very beginning, the United States was inclined to support the Allied cause. Most Americans sympathized with the Allies, and many provided monetary and moral support for relatives living in England and France. President Wilson and many of his advisors had close ties with British diplomats. As the war went on, American economic ties with the Allies, especially England, became even stronger. England relied more and more on goods from America as European economies went into decline, and the English blockade of German ports meant that it was much less profitable and more difficult to trade with Germany.

Remaining neutral toward Germany also became increasingly difficult. Americans' feelings toward the Germans had hardened during the first years of the war, when German submarine attacks damaged neutral shipping and when newspapers reported on German atrocities in neutral Belgium. In early 1917 Germany stepped up submarine attacks once more; at that point, the U.S. entrance into the war became almost inevitable.

Did you know . . .

- The American economy boomed between 1914 and 1917. According to historian Daniel M. Smith, author of *The Great Departure: The United States and World War I, 1914–1920*, the value of American goods shipped overseas rose from $500 million in 1914 to $3.5 billion in 1917. America built a powerful weapons industry, and trade with the Allied countries nearly doubled from what it had been during peacetime.

- Many Americans wanted to serve in the war even though the United States had declared its neutrality. Some, such as poet Alan Seeger, joined the French foreign legion, a branch of the French army that accepted foreigners. Others served as ambulance drivers or medics with the Red Cross, an international aid agency. Famous American authors Ernest Hemingway, William Faulkner, and John Dos Passos all participated in some kind of alternative service in the war.

For More Information

Books

Clare, John D., ed. *First World War.* San Diego, CA: Harcourt Brace, 1995.

Esposito, David M. *The Legacy of Woodrow Wilson: American War Aims in World War I.* Westport, CT: Praeger, 1996.

Jannen, William, Jr. *Lions of July: How Men Who Wanted Peace Went to War in 1914.* Novato, CA: Presidio, 1996.

Kennedy, David M. *Over Here: The First World War and American Society.* New York: Oxford University Press, 1980.

Kent, Zachary. *World War I: "The War to End Wars."* Hillside, NJ: Enslow, 1994.

Link, Arthur Stanley. *Woodrow Wilson: Revolution, War, and Peace.* Arlington Heights, IL: AHM Publishing, 1979.

Osinski, Alice. *Woodrow Wilson: Twenty-Eighth President of the United States.* Chicago: Children's Press, 1989.

Rogers, James T. *Woodrow Wilson: Visionary for Peace.* New York: Facts on File, 1997.

Ross, Stewart. *Causes and Consequences of World War I.* Austin, TX: Raintree Steck-Vaughn, 1998.

Smith, Daniel M. *The Great Departure: The United States and World War I, 1914–1920.* New York: McGraw-Hill, 1965.

Articles

Wilson, Woodrow. *Message to Congress,* 63rd Cong., 2d sess., Senate Doc. 566. Washington D.C.: Government Printing Office, 1914, pp. 3–4.

Web sites

"Neutrality: Woodrow Wilson, Appeal for Neutrality." [Online] http://www.iath.virginia.edu/seminar/unit10/wilson1.htm (accessed April 2001).

World War I Document Archive. [Online] http://www.lib.byu.edu/~rdh/wwi/1914/wilsonneut.html (accessed February 2001).

Woodrow Wilson's War Message

Delivered to a special session of Congress on April 2, 1917

Reprinted from the World War I Document Archive, available online at http://www.lib.byu.edu/ ~rdh/wwi/1917 /wilswarm.html

When the major European nations entered into World War I in the summer of 1914, most of America was united in the desire to avoid getting involved in the conflict. Shortly after the war began, President Woodrow Wilson announced his intention to keep America neutral in thought and deed, for he hoped that America might play a vital role in bringing the warring nations to peace. But neutrality (the policy of not getting involved in the fighting) proved more difficult than anyone had anticipated.

As World War I wore on, the United States found itself increasingly compelled to take sides. Most Americans sympathized with the French and British, who appeared to be the victims of German aggression and brutality. And trade with France and Britain boomed during the war, as those countries grew increasingly dependent on American goods. Trade and cultural ties were important factors linking the United States to the Allies, but these things alone would not have been enough to draw the United States into the war. The single biggest factor driving the United States into war was German aggression.

"Our motive will not be revenge or the victorious assertion of the physical might of the nation, but only the vindication of right, of human right, of which we are only a single champion."

Woodrow Wilson

A German submarine attack sunk the British passenger ship *Lusitania* on May 7, 1915, killing 1,198 people on board, including 128 Americans. This incident increased awareness of the European war in the still-neutral U.S. *(Corbis Corporation. Reproduced by permission.)*

German military leaders recognized that to win the war they had to damage the economies of France and England. Their strategy was to stop supplies from reaching those countries, just as the British blockade of German ports stopped supplies from entering Germany. Early in the war German submarines launched numerous attacks on ships bringing supplies to the Allies. America protested loudly, and because the Germans did not want America to enter the war they stopped the attacks. By January 1917, however, the Germans decided that the only way for them to win the war was to resume unrestricted submarine warfare on neutral shipping. When German subs sank three U.S. ships in March 1917, President Wilson had had enough. He went to Congress and asked for a declaration of war on Germany on April 2, 1917.

Wilson did not make his decision lightly. As the following excerpt from his speech to Congress shows, he carefully explained why he believed America should enter into the war. Wilson expressed outrage at recent German submarine attacks and explained why the United States must not endure these attacks; he detailed how the United States should prepare itself for war and outlined the goals that America hoped to attain by going to war. In one of the most striking passages from the speech, Wilson states that America must fight "for the rights of nations great and small and the privilege of men everywhere to choose their way of life and of obedience. The world must be made safe for democracy." This statement helped shape American foreign policy for the remainder of the twentieth century.

Things to remember while reading President Wilson's War Message:

- The British navy created a strong blockade of German ports on the North Sea early in the war. This blockade made it very difficult for Germany to import food, clothes, and other essential supplies. As the war continued and German farmers could no longer provide enough food for the German people, the blockade threatened to literally starve Germany to death. German submarine attacks on ships traveling to England were meant to inflict similar hardships on the British.

- In his speech, Wilson complains that submarine attacks defy the laws of humanity and the laws of war at sea. The rules of warfare required an attacker to notify a ship before attacking it. German diplomats contended that this rule should not apply to submarines, because submarines depended on surprise for their effectiveness and were very vulnerable to attack when they surfaced. By World War II, when every country had submarines, it was widely accepted that submarines would launch surprise attacks on ships.

- According to the U.S. Constitution, only Congress may declare war. The president, as commander in chief of U.S. military forces, asks Congress to declare war.

- Though Wilson focuses on German submarine attacks as the major reason for going to war, the "Zimmermann telegram" also influenced America's decision to enter the war. In the Zimmermann telegram, a leading German diplomat proposed to Mexico that it join with Germany and attack the United States. The Americans intercepted and published the telegram, which stirred up anti-German sentiment.

War Message

I have called the Congress into extraordinary session because there are serious, very serious, choices of policy to be made, and made immediately, which it was neither right nor constitutionally permissible that I should assume the responsibility of making.

*On the 3d of February last I officially laid before you the extraordinary announcement of the Imperial German Government that on and after the 1st day of February it was its purpose to put aside all restraints of law or of humanity and use its submarines to sink every vessel that sought to approach either the ports of Great Britain and Ireland or the western coasts of Europe or any of the ports controlled by the enemies of Germany within the Mediterranean. . . . The new policy has swept every restriction aside. Vessels of every kind, whatever their flag, their character, their cargo, their destination, their errand, have been ruthlessly sent to the bottom without warning and without thought of help or mercy for those on board, the vessels of friendly neutrals along with those of **belligerents**. . . .*

*I was for a little while unable to believe that such things would in fact be done by any government that had hitherto subscribed to the humane practices of civilized nations. International law had its origin in the attempt to set up some law which would be respected and observed upon the seas, where no nation had **right of dominion** and where lay the free highways of the world. . . . This **minimum of right** the German Government has swept aside under the plea of retaliation and necessity and because it had no weapons which it could use at sea except these which it is impossible to employ as it is employing them without throwing to the winds all scruples of humanity or of respect for the understandings that were supposed to underlie the intercourse of the world. I am not now thinking of the loss of property involved, immense and serious as that is, but only of the wanton and wholesale destruction of the lives of noncombatants, men, women, and children, engaged in pursuits which have always, even in the darkest periods of modern history, been deemed innocent and legitimate. Property can be paid for; the lives of peaceful and innocent people can not be. The present German submarine warfare against commerce is a warfare against mankind.*

Belligerent: A participant in a fight or war.

Right of dominion: Legal claim; Wilson is referring to the fact that beyond a certain distance from the coast, the oceans are owned by no country.

Minimum of right: Minimal standards for how to treat other ships at sea.

*It is a war against all nations. American ships have been sunk, American lives taken, in ways which it has stirred us very deeply to learn of, but the ships and people of other neutral and friendly nations have been sunk and overwhelmed in the waters in the same way. There has been no discrimination. The challenge is to all mankind. Each nation must decide for itself how it will meet it. The choice we make for ourselves must be made with a **moderation of counsel and a temperateness of judgment** befitting our character and our motives as a nation. We must put excited feeling away. Our motive will not be revenge or the victorious assertion of the physical might of the nation, but only the vindication of right, of human right, of which we are only a single champion.*

*When I addressed the Congress on the 26th of February last, I thought that it would suffice to assert our neutral rights with arms, our right to use the seas against unlawful interference, our right to keep our people safe against unlawful violence. But armed neutrality, it now appears, is **impracticable**. . .. There is one choice we can not make, we are incapable of making: we will not choose the path of submission and suffer the most sacred rights of our nation and our people to be ignored or violated. The wrongs against which we now **array** ourselves are no common wrongs; they cut to the very roots of human life.*

With a profound sense of the solemn and even tragical character of the step I am taking and of the grave responsibilities which it involves, but in unhesitating obedience to what I deem my constitutional duty, I advise that the Congress declare the recent course of the Imperial German Government to be in fact nothing less than war against the Government and people of the United States; that it [Congress] formally accept the status of belligerent which has thus been thrust upon it, and that it take immediate steps not only to put the country in a more thorough state of defense but also to exert all its power and employ all its resources to bring the Government of the German Empire to terms and end the war.

What this will involve is clear. It will involve the utmost practicable cooperation in counsel and action with the governments now at war with Germany, and, as incident to that, the extension to those governments of the most liberal financial credits, in order that our resources may so far as possible be added to theirs. It will involve the organization and mobilization of all the material resources of the country to supply the materials of war and serve the incidental needs of the nation in the most abundant and yet the most economical and

Moderation of counsel and a temperateness of judgment: Wilson is trying to stress that his decision to go to war is rational and carefully thought out; he is trying to contrast America's "moderation" and "temperateness" with the aggression of Germany.

Impracticable: Not possible.

Array: Order or organize.

efficient way possible. It will involve the immediate full equipment of the Navy in all respects but particularly in supplying it with the best means of dealing with the enemy's submarines. It will involve the immediate addition to the armed forces of the United States . . . at least 500,000 men, who should, in my opinion, be chosen upon the principle of **universal liability to service**, and also the authorization of subsequent additional **increments of equal force** so soon as they may be needed and can be handled in training. It will involve also, of course, the **granting of adequate credits** to the Government, sustained, I hope, so far as they can equitably be sustained by the present generation, by well conceived taxation. . . .

While we do these things, these deeply momentous things, let us be very clear, and make very clear to all the world what our motives and our objects are. . . . Our object . . . is to **vindicate** the principles of peace and justice in the life of the world as against selfish and **autocratic** power and to set up amongst the really free and self-governed peoples of the world such a **concert** of purpose and of action as will henceforth ensure the observance of those principles. Neutrality is no longer feasible or desirable where the peace of the world is involved and the freedom of its peoples, and the menace to that peace and freedom lies in the existence of autocratic governments backed by organized force which is controlled wholly by their will, not by the will of their people. We have seen the last of neutrality in such circumstances. We are at the beginning of an age in which it will be insisted that the same standards of conduct and of responsibility for wrong done shall be observed among nations and their governments that are observed among the individual citizens of civilized states. . . .

We are accepting this challenge of hostile purpose because we know that in [the present German government] . . . we can never have a friend; and that in the presence of its organized power, always lying in wait to accomplish we know not what purpose, there can be no assured security for the democratic governments of the world. We are now about to accept **gage** of battle with this natural foe to liberty and shall, if necessary, spend the whole force of the nation to check and nullify its pretensions and its power. We are glad, now that we see the facts with no veil of false **pretence** about them, to fight thus for the ultimate peace of the world and for the liberation of its peoples, the German peoples included: for the rights of nations great and small and the privilege of men everywhere to choose their way of life and of obedience. The world must be made safe for democracy. Its peace must be planted upon the tested foundations of political liberty.

Universal liability to service: Wilson is calling for the selection of soldiers from men within a specified age range; the result of this call was the random selection, or draft, of soldiers from the general population.

Increments of equal force: Groups of troops.

Granting of adequate credits: Wilson is saying that the government will need to raise money—"adequate credits"—to pay for its army; it will raise money by raising taxes and by selling bonds (financial certificates that guarantee repayment of the sum the buyer pays plus interest).

Vindicate: To remove doubt.

Autocratic: An autocrat is a single powerful leader; here "autocratic" means without regard for the interests of the people.

Concert: Joint effort.

Gage: Challenge.

Pretence: Pretending or deception; usually spelled "pretense" in the United States.

*We have no selfish ends to serve. **We desire no conquest, no dominion.** We seek no **indemnities** for ourselves, no material compensation for the sacrifices we shall freely make. We are but one of the champions of the rights of mankind. We shall be satisfied when those rights have been made as secure as the faith and the freedom of nations can make them. . . .*

*It will be all the easier for us to conduct ourselves as belligerents in a high spirit of right and fairness because we act **without animus, not in enmity** towards a people or with the desire to bring any injury or disadvantage upon them, but only in armed opposition to an irresponsible government which has thrown aside all considerations of humanity and of right and is running amuck. We are, let me say again, **the sincere friends of the German people,** and shall desire nothing so much as the early reestablishment of intimate relations of mutual advantage between us — however hard it may be for them, for the time being, to believe that this is spoken from our hearts. . . .*

It is a distressing and oppressive duty, gentlemen of the Congress, which I have performed in thus addressing you. There are, it may be, many months of fiery trial and sacrifice ahead of us. It is a fearful thing to lead this great peaceful people into war, into the most terrible and disastrous of all wars, civilization itself seeming to be in the balance. But the right is more precious than peace, and we shall fight for the things which we have always carried nearest our hearts—for democracy, for the right of those who submit to authority to have a voice in their own governments, for the rights and liberties of small nations, for a universal dominion of right by such a concert of free peoples as shall bring peace and safety to all nations and make the world itself at last free. To such a task we can dedicate our lives and our fortunes, everything that we are and everything that we have, with the pride of those who know that the day has come when America is privileged to spend her blood and her might for the principles that gave her birth and happiness and the peace which she has treasured. God helping her, she can do no other.

We desire no conquest, no dominion: Wilson is assuring the world that America is not entering the war to gain territory or power for itself.

Indemnities: Security against losses suffered.

Without animus, not in enmity: Without ill will or hatred; notice that Wilson often uses paired terms when he wants to emphasize his point.

The sincere friends of the German people: Wilson is trying to emphasize that the United States is fighting against the government of Germany, which he believes does not represent the will of the German people. This is both an effort to appeal to the people of Germany and to appeal to Americans not to harass German Americans and/or German immigrants living in the United States.

What happened next . . .

The United States Congress declared war on Germany on April 6, 1917. French and British soldiers and citizens cele-

A *New York Journal* headline marks the entrance of the United States into World War I, April 6, 1917.
(Corbis Corporation. Reproduced by permission.)

brated, for they felt sure that America's entrance into the conflict would turn the tide of the war. It took some time for their hopes to be realized, however. America was slow bringing its troops into action. It had to enlist, train, and equip an army, and it took months to do so. The first U.S. forces began arriving in Europe late in 1917, but it wasn't until the summer of 1918 that a strong American army was ready to fight. Allied troops withstood the last German offensive in the spring of 1918 and, with the help of fresh, well-supplied American forces, they struck the Germans hard through the summer and into the fall of 1918. American soldiers under General John "Black Jack" Pershing fought well in major battles at Saint-Mihiel, Belleau Wood, and the Meuse-Argonne Region. On November 11, 1918, the Germans surrendered. The American presence had proved to be the key factor in ending a war that had lasted four years and had laid waste to major sections of France, Belgium, and several other countries.

Did you know . . .

- The move from neutrality to war brought real changes in the United States. The government passed strict laws forbidding any words or actions that questioned the government's war aims, and it created a government agency, the Committee on Public Information, to produce propaganda promoting government policies.

- Wilson's decision to institute a military draft (required enrollment in the military for selected people) in 1917 was quite unpopular, even within the military. Many people believed that military drafts were incompatible with democracy. Despite these problems, the draft successfully built an army of nearly one million soldiers.

For More Information

Books

Clare, John D., ed. *First World War*. San Diego, CA: Harcourt Brace, 1995.

Esposito, David M. *The Legacy of Woodrow Wilson: American War Aims in World War I*. Westport, CT: Praeger, 1996.

Jannen, William, Jr. *Lions of July: How Men Who Wanted Peace Went to War in 1914*. Novato, CA: Presidio, 1996.

Kennedy, David M. *Over Here: The First World War and American Society*. New York: Oxford University Press, 1980.

Kent, Zachary. *World War I: "The War to End Wars."* Hillside, NJ: Enslow, 1994.

Link, Arthur Stanley. *Woodrow Wilson: Revolution, War, and Peace*. Arlington Heights, IL: AHM Publishing, 1979.

Osinski, Alice. *Woodrow Wilson: Twenty-Eighth President of the United States*. Chicago: Children's Press, 1989.

Rogers, James T. *Woodrow Wilson: Visionary for Peace*. New York: Facts on File, 1997.

Ross, Stewart. *Causes and Consequences of World War I*. Austin, TX: Raintree Steck-Vaughn, 1998.

Smith, Daniel M. *The Great Departure: The United States and World War I, 1914–1920*. New York: McGraw-Hill, 1965.

Articles

Wilson, Woodrow. *War Messages,* 65th Cong., 1st sess., Senate Doc. 5, serial 7264. (Washington, DC: Government Printing Office, 1917), pp. 3–8.

Web sites

World War I Document Archive. [Online] http://www.lib.byu.edu/~rdh/wwi/1917/wilswarm.html (accessed February 2001).

Woodrow Wilson's Fourteen Points

Delivered in a Joint Session of Congress, January 8, 1918

Reprinted from the World War I Document Archive, available online at http://www.lib.byu.edu/~rdh/wwi/1918/14points.html

Woodrow Wilson led the American people into World War I not just to win the war but also to win the peace—that is, to create peacetime conditions that would rule out war in the future. Wilson hated war; it violated his moral and religious principles and caused innocent people undue suffering. Wilson also hated war because it disrupted the international trade that kept America strong. Wilson believed that America and other nations would be best served if countries could settle their disputes without war and continue to trade peacefully. Long before the war ended, Wilson began arguing for peace terms that would establish more orderly relations among the world's major countries. He expressed his vision of the postwar world most clearly in his Fourteen Points address, which he delivered before Congress on January 8, 1918.

Wilson's Fourteen Points established some basic principles for making peace. The Fourteen Points can be broken down into several sections. The first five points proposed general rules governing the behavior of all warring parties. They called for "open covenants of peace, openly arrived at" (as a protection against secret treaties), freedom of the seas, free

"What we demand in this war, therefore, is nothing peculiar to ourselves. It is that the world be made fit and safe to live in; and particularly that it be made safe for every peace-loving nation. . . ."

Woodrow Wilson

Woodrow Wilson: Visionary of Peace or Progressive Politician?

Woodrow Wilson is best known for his leadership of the United States during World War I and for his dramatic statements about the need for world peace. However, he spent most of his political career campaigning for reforms (policy changes) in the United States. Wilson was known as a progressive politician, which meant that he favored reforms in American government that were designed to limit the power of corporations, provide **basic protections** for consumers, and give common people a bigger role in their government. He was part of a generation of politicians who had great influence on American government from 1900 to 1920.

Wilson was born in 1856, the son of a highly educated Presbyterian minister. He was a slow learner, not learning to read until he was almost twelve years old, but he developed quickly in high school and became a popular public speaker and athlete while attending Princeton University in New Jersey. Wilson later studied law and history, earning a doctorate degree in history from Johns Hopkins University in 1885. Wilson became a professor at Princeton University and later became the president of Princeton. His success as a university president launched him on his political career.

Wilson was elected as the Democratic governor of New Jersey in 1910. During his two years in office he pushed through progressive laws that gave voters a stronger voice in electing state officials, regulated public utilities like electricity and gas, reorganized the school system, established workmen's compensation (payment for on-the-job injuries), and fought corruption in state politics. His strengths as governor brought him national acclaim and earned him the Democratic presidential nomination in 1912.

Wilson campaigned on a platform of reforms he called "The New Freedom." He beat incumbent president William Howard Taft, former president Theodore Roosevelt, and Socialist candidate Eugene V. Debs to become president in 1912. Within just a few years the major elements of Wilson's "New Freedom" plan were passed into law: child labor restrictions; laws establishing better working conditions

Basic protections: Laws protecting people from faulty products.

trade among nations, smaller armies, and new negotiations on colonial holdings that respected the people in those colonies. Points six through thirteen proposed specific territorial adjustments, most of which were interpreted as punishments for members of the Central Powers. These points granted territory for sailors and railroad workers; a progressive income tax; the Federal Reserve System to regulate the nation's banks; and the Federal Trade Commission to prevent unfair monopolies in business. But Wilson's domestic accomplishments would soon be overshadowed by the war in Europe.

When World War I started in Europe in 1914, President Woodrow Wilson had conflicting goals: He wanted to keep the United States neutral and try to end the war by acting as a mediator. But he also wanted to protect the rights of Americans to trade wherever they chose. For nearly three years Wilson kept the United States neutral. But when German submarines began to attack U.S. ships in an effort to prevent supplies from reaching Britain, Wilson felt that he could no longer keep America out of the war.

Though Wilson led his country into war alongside the Allies on April 6, 1917, he continued to promote his vision of a more peaceful world. Wilson believed that strong trade and open communications between countries would make war

unnecessary. In several speeches Wilson expressed his vision of a peaceful postwar world; his most famous speech is known as the Fourteen Points address. Among the points was a call for an international organization dedicated to keeping peace between nations; Wilson called it the League of Nations.

Pushing for the United States to join the League of Nations was Wilson's political and personal downfall. Many Americans were not willing to become involved in world politics; they believed that the United States was better off making political decisions based solely on her own needs. Wilson spent his physical health and his political power promoting the idea of the League of Nations; but the Senate rejected the treaty that called for U.S. participation in the league, and Wilson's political party lost the presidential election of 1920. Wilson died on February 3, 1924. Rarely in American history have presidents made such an impact on both domestic and foreign policy. Wilson is widely considered to be one of the greatest presidents of the twentieth century.

to France and Italy, granted autonomy (self-rule) to the peoples of the Austro-Hungarian empire and Ottoman Empire, and established an independent Poland. The fourteenth point—key to Wilson's view of the postwar world—called for the creation of an international organization to settle disputes between countries. This League of Nations, as it came to be called, was the most radical of Wilson's proposals and later met with intense opposition in the United States.

Things to remember while reading Woodrow Wilson's Fourteen Points:

- The Fourteen Points address came well before the end of the war, and before the United States had played a major role in the fighting. Germany reacted with anger at the suggestion that she give up so much, and some historians believe that the Fourteen Points kept the Germans fighting longer than they might have otherwise.

- Wilson's Fourteen Points address gained him a great deal of support in the United States and overseas, for it seemed to indicate that the president was truly looking out for the good of the world and would avoid the kind of secret treaties that had started the war in the first place. After this speech, Wilson became the most respected spokesman for Allied war efforts.

Woodrow Wilson's Fourteen Points

Gentlemen of the Congress:

Once more, as repeatedly before, the spokesmen of the Central Empires have indicated their desire to discuss the objects of the war and the possible basis of a general peace. . . .

. . .[T]hey have again attempted to acquaint the world with their objects in the war and have again challenged their adversaries to say what their objects are and what sort of settlement they would deem just and satisfactory. There is no good reason why that challenge should not be responded to, and responded to with the utmost candor. We did not wait for it. Not once, but again and again, we have laid our whole thought and purpose before the world, not in general terms only, but each time with sufficient definition to make it clear what sort of definite terms of settlement must necessarily spring out of them. . . .

It will be our wish and purpose that the processes of peace, when they are begun, shall be absolutely open and that they shall involve and permit henceforth no secret understandings of any kind. The day of conquest and **aggrandizement** is gone by; so is also the day of secret **covenants** entered into in the interest of particular governments and likely at some unlooked-for moment to upset the peace of the world. It is this happy fact, now clear to the view of every public man whose thoughts do not still linger in an age that is dead and gone, which makes it possible for every nation whose purposes are consistent with justice and the peace of the world to **avow** now or at any other time the objects it has in view.

We entered this war because violations of right had occurred which touched us to the quick and made the life of our own people impossible unless they were corrected and the world secure once for all against their recurrence. What we demand in this war, therefore, is nothing peculiar to ourselves. It is that the world be made fit and safe to live in; and particularly that it be made safe for every peace-loving nation which, like our own, wishes to live its own life, determine its own insti-

The American delegation at the Versailles Peace Conference in Versailles, France, December 1918. Woodrow Wilson is seated center. *(Corbis Corporation. Reproduced by permission.)*

Aggrandizement: Increasing power and influence.

Covenants: Agreements or treaties, such as those that bound European nations to go to war.

Avow: Openly state.

tutions, be assured of justice and fair dealing by the other peoples of the world as against force and selfish aggression. All the peoples of the world are in effect partners in this interest, and for our own part we see very clearly that unless justice be done to others it will not be done to us. The program of the world's peace, therefore, is our program; and that program, the only possible program, as we see it, is this:

I. Open covenants of peace, openly arrived at, after which there shall be no private international understandings of any kind but diplomacy shall proceed always frankly and in the public view.

II. Absolute freedom of navigation upon the seas, outside territorial waters, alike in peace and in war, except as the seas may be closed in whole or in part by international action for the enforcement of international covenants.

III. The removal, so far as possible, of all economic barriers and the establishment of an equality of trade conditions among all the nations consenting to the peace and associating themselves for its maintenance.

IV. Adequate guarantees given and taken that national armaments will be reduced to the lowest point consistent with domestic safety.

*V. A free, open-minded, and absolutely impartial adjustment of all **colonial claims**, based upon a strict observance of the principle that in determining all such questions of **sovereignty** the interests of the populations concerned must have equal weight with the equitable claims of the government whose title is to be determined.*

*VI. The evacuation of all Russian territory and such a settlement of all questions affecting Russia as will secure the best and freest cooperation of the other nations of the world in obtaining for **her** an **unhampered and unembarrassed** opportunity for the independent determination of her own political development and national policy and assure her of a sincere welcome into the society of free nations under **institutions** of her own choosing; and, more than a welcome, assistance also of every kind that she may need and may herself desire. The treatment accorded Russia by her sister nations in the months to come will be the **acid test** of their good will, of their comprehension of her needs as distinguished from their own interests, and of their intelligent and unselfish sympathy.*

VII. Belgium, the whole world will agree, must be evacuated and restored, without any attempt to limit the sovereignty which she

Colonial claims: Claims to colonies in distant locations such as Africa and the Pacific.

Sovereignty: Authority over a country; Wilson wanted colonies to be given more say over how they were governed; this is called "popular sovereignty," or the rule of the people.

Her: Russia.

Unhampered and unembarrassed: Unrestricted and free from shame; again, Wilson uses a pair of like terms to make his point, which is that the Russian people should be allowed to choose their government without outside interference.

Institutions: Forms of government.

Acid test: A test that reveals the true quality.

enjoys in common with all other free nations. No other single act will serve as this will serve to restore confidence among the nations in the laws which they have themselves set and determined for the government of their relations with one another. Without this healing act the whole structure and validity of international law is forever impaired.

VIII. All French territory should be freed and the invaded portions restored, and the wrong done to France by Prussia in 1871 **in the matter of Alsace-Lorraine,** which has unsettled the peace of the world for nearly fifty years, should be righted, in order that peace may once more be made secure in the interest of all.

IX. A readjustment of the frontiers of Italy should be effected along clearly recognizable lines of nationality.

X. The peoples of Austria-Hungary, whose place among the nations we wish to see safeguarded and assured, should be accorded the freest opportunity to **autonomous** development.

XI. **Rumania,** Serbia, and Montenegro should be evacuated; occupied territories restored; Serbia accorded free and secure access to the sea; and the relations of the several Balkan states to one another determined by friendly counsel along historically established lines of allegiance and nationality; and international guarantees of the political and economic independence and **territorial integrity** of the several Balkan states should be entered into.

XII. The Turkish portion of the present Ottoman Empire should be assured a secure sovereignty, but the other nationalities which are now under Turkish rule should be assured an undoubted security of life and an absolutely **unmolested** opportunity of autonomous development, and the **Dardanelles** should be permanently opened as a free passage to the ships and commerce of all nations under international **guarantees.**

XIII. An independent Polish state should be erected which should include the territories inhabited by indisputably Polish populations, which should be assured a free and secure access to the sea, and whose political and economic independence and territorial integrity should be guaranteed by international covenant.

XIV. A general association of nations must be formed under specific covenants for the purpose of affording mutual guarantees of political independence and territorial integrity to great and small states alike.

In the matter of Alsace-Lorraine: Alsace-Lorraine is a region that was taken from France by Germany (formerly called Prussia) in 1871; the French had long believed that they should get the territory back, and they did at the end of World War I.

Autonomous: Independent; without the interference of the Austro-Hungarian empire.

Rumania: Romania.

Territorial integrity: This phrase refers to the rightful borders of the various Balkan countries, a matter that was in dispute for much of the twentieth century.

Unmolested: Unbothered; as before, Wilson is indicating his preference that the people of a country or region be allowed to determine their own political future without the interference of others.

Dardanelles: A strait between Europe and Turkey in Asia, connecting the Aegean Sea and the Sea of Marmara.

Guarantees: Treaties or agreements; in this case, those that protect the rights of ships on the sea.

*In regard to these essential **rectifications** of wrong and assertions of right we feel ourselves to be intimate partners of all the governments and peoples associated together against the **Imperialists**. We cannot be separated in interest or divided in purpose. We stand together until the end. . . . We have no jealousy of German greatness, and there is nothing in this program that impairs it. We **grudge** her no achievement or **distinction of learning or of pacific enterprise** such as have made her record very bright and very enviable. We do not wish to injure her or to block in any way her legitimate influence or power. We do not wish to fight her either with arms or with hostile arrangements of trade if she is willing to associate herself with us and the other peace-loving nations of the world in covenants of justice and law and fair dealing. We wish her only to accept a place of equality among the peoples of the world—the new world in which we now live—instead of a place of mastery.*

We have spoken now, surely, in terms too concrete to admit of any further doubt or question. An evident principle runs through the whole program I have outlined. It is the principle of justice to all peoples and nationalities, and their right to live on equal terms of liberty and safety with one another, whether they be strong or weak.

*Unless this principle be made its foundation no part of the structure of international justice can stand. The people of the United States could act upon no other principle; and to the **vindication** of this principle they are ready to devote their lives, their honor, and everything they possess. The moral climax of this the **culminating** and final war for human liberty has come, and they are ready to put their own strength, their own highest purpose, their own integrity and devotion to the test.*

What happened next . . .

With the help of the United States, the Allies went on to win the war, and Wilson's Fourteen Points provided the framework for the Treaty of Versailles, the major treaty that settled issues between the warring nations. However, the treaty was not nearly as fair as Wilson had hoped; it split up territories among the victorious European powers and punished Germany severely. The Treaty of Versailles was also the cause of

Wilson's political downfall. The treaty, which Wilson helped to write, called for the United States to become part of the League of Nations. Wilson and his supporters—called internationalists—believed that America's future prosperity would lie in global trade. They thought that the United States should protect its economic interests overseas by cooperating with other countries to avoid warfare and other disruptions of trade. Wilson's opponents—who dominated the Senate—were known as isolationists. They believed that the United States was better off avoiding entanglements with foreign countries and that America should concentrate on building up its domestic economy.

Isolationist senators were dead set against America joining the League of Nations, and they took their campaign to the American people. Wilson did the same, traveling around the country promoting his peace plan. In the end the Senate was too strong and Wilson too weak. The Senate defeated the Treaty of Versailles, which meant that America would not

Newspapers announce the surrender of Germany, thus ending World War I on November 8, 1918.
(Corbis Corporation. Reproduced by permission.)

President Wilson kicks off his campaign to promote the Treaty of Versailles—which includes a stipulation that the U.S. join the League of Nations—in Columbus, Ohio, on September 5, 1919. *(Corbis Corporation. Reproduced by permission.)*

enter the League of Nations. Many historians see America's refusal to join the League of Nations as a contributing factor in the coming of World War II. If it had joined the league, they believe, America might have been able to stop the rise of Hitler's Germany. In 1945 the United States did join an international organization designed to promote world peace, the United Nations.

Did you know . . .

- Campaigning for the Treaty of Versailles nearly killed President Woodrow Wilson. While on a whirlwind speaking tour of the United States to drum up support for the treaty, Wilson suffered a stroke and was virtually incapacitated for several months. He never fully recovered his health and left office in 1921 a broken man.

- Several of Wilson's ideas for the peace treaty were rejected. Germany was punished far more severely than Wilson had wished, and France and England profited more than Wilson had intended.

- Though American troops stopped fighting in November 1918 along with everybody else, it took until July 1921 for the United States Congress to pass a simple declaration stating that America's war with Germany was over.

For More Information

Books

Clare, John D., ed. *First World War.* San Diego, CA: Harcourt Brace, 1995.

Esposito, David M. *The Legacy of Woodrow Wilson: American War Aims in World War I.* Westport, CT: Praeger, 1996.

Jannen, William, Jr. *Lions of July: How Men Who Wanted Peace Went to War in 1914.* Novato, CA: Presidio, 1996.

Kennedy, David M. *Over Here: The First World War and American Society.* New York: Oxford University Press, 1980.

Kent, Zachary. *World War I: "The War to End Wars."* Hillside, NJ: Enslow, 1994.

Link, Arthur Stanley. *Woodrow Wilson: Revolution, War, and Peace.* Arlington Heights, IL: AHM Publishing, 1979.

Osinski, Alice. *Woodrow Wilson: Twenty-Eighth President of the United States.* Chicago: Children's Press, 1989.

Rogers, James T. *Woodrow Wilson: Visionary for Peace.* New York: Facts on File, 1997.

Ross, Stewart. *Causes and Consequences of World War I.* Austin, TX: Raintree Steck-Vaughn, 1998.

Smith, Daniel M. *The Great Departure: The United States and World War I, 1914–1920.* New York: McGraw-Hill, 1965.

Articles

Wilson, Woodrow. "Speech on the Fourteen Points," 65th Cong., 2d sess., *Congressional Record* (8 January 1918), pp. 680–81.

Web sites

World War I Document Archive.[Online] http://www.lib.byu.edu/ ~rdh/wwi/1918/14points.html (accessed February 2001).

Literature of the Great War

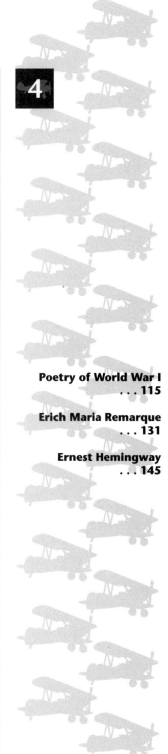

4

W orld War I stimulated some of the greatest writing of the twentieth century. Not only did it produce a great out-pouring of poetry during the course of the fighting, but it also spawned several war novels that now have a place among the great books of the world. Most of the "war poets," as they were known, came from England, which sent a great number of highly educated men into war with its volunteer army. Among the most famous of these poets are **Rupert Brooke** (1887–1915), **Wilfred Owen** (1893–1918), and **Siegfried Sassoon** (1886–1967). American poet **Alan Seeger** (1888–1916) also contributed an important volume of poetry about the war. Each of these poets is represented in the section on war poetry that follows.

Writers who expressed their thoughts about the war through fiction came from many countries. Though there are many great novels and memoirs written about the war, included here are excerpts from two of the greatest: *All Quiet on the Western Front* by German novelist **Erich Maria Remarque** (1898–1970), and *A Farewell to Arms* by American novelist **Ernest Hemingway** (1899–1961). Both of these novels were published a decade after the end of the war; both address the impact that the war had on the world. (Both books have been made into movies several times; *All Quiet on the Western Front* won an Academy Award for Best Picture in 1930.)

World War I had a huge influence on the way people thought of the world, and that impact is clearly visible in the literature of the war. Before the war, people in England, France, Germany, and the United States (as well as other combatant countries) generally trusted in their governments and believed that it was an honor to die for one's country. There was also a widely held view that society was progressing and that the rise of modern society would bring an end to misery and warfare. World War I ended most such dreams of human progress; people were bitterly disappointed that technological and economic progress did not mean social and political progress. In fact, technology had only been used to increase the scale of killing.

Novelists and poets alike responded to the war by creating works that ponder the deeper meanings of the war and its effects on men and women. These writers suggested that men and women had become alienated, or distanced, from the ideas of honor and glory that had motivated the generations that came before them. Postwar writers felt that the modern experience was something altogether new, and through their writing they tried to understand what ideals a person could hold in the midst of world conflict. These writers were part of a literary movement called Modernism, which was the dominant literary mode for the next fifty years, until roughly the 1960s.

Literature poses questions about the war that are raised by few other sources. Generals think about troop movements and strategy, politicians think about peace treaties and social programs, but writers ponder deep questions about the meaning of life. As you read the sections that follow, think of the questions raised by these works. What did the experience of combat do to people? How did the stories of war glory and honor match up with the actual experience of combat? Was there, in fact, any glory to war? These are some of the questions posed by the war poets quoted in the first section of this chapter, **Poetry of World War I**. Hemingway and Remarque explore different topics. Both seem to ask, How is an individual to behave in a world gone mad? To whom does one owe loyalty? To whom must one be true? Above all else, these novelists and poets force one to consider how people are to retain their humanity in the midst of the chaos and horror of modern warfare.

Poetry of World War I

For the soldiers who went off to fight in World War I, literature was the main form of entertainment. "In 1914 there was virtually no cinema," writes historian Paul Fussell in *The Great War and Modern Memory*; there was no radio at all; and there was certainly no television. Fussell continues, "Amusement was largely found in language formally arranged, either in books and periodicals or at the theater and music hall, or in one's own or one's friends' anecdotes, rumors, or clever structuring of words." For British soldiers in particular, writing poetry was one of the chief sources of pleasure. Britain formed its army with volunteers, and many of these volunteers came out of Great Britain's high-quality public school system, the British equivalent of private preparatory high schools and col-

I have a rendezvous with Death/ At some disputed barricade,/ When Spring comes back with rustling shade/ And apple-blossoms fill the air—/ I have a rendezvous with Death/ When Spring brings back blue days and fair.

From I Have A Rendezvous with Death *by Alan Seeger*

Rupert Brooke (1887–1915)

English poet Rupert Brooke is perhaps the most famous of the patriotic poets, poets who celebrated England's entry into World War I. Born on August 3, 1887, to a family of educators, Brooke excelled at school. He became part of a circle of poets at Cambridge University who rebelled against the poetry of their parents' generation and hoped to create new verses that were realistic, bold, and vital. They were known as the Georgian poets. Brooke published his first collection of poems in 1911 and made his name by contributing to *Georgian Poetry*, a book containing selected works by different poets, published in 1912.

Like many other educated young Englishmen, Brooke responded to the declaration of war in 1914 with patriotic fervor. He had tired of "a world grown old and cold and weary" and hoped to find glory in the war. His sonnets (fourteen-line poems) about the thrill of going off to war to fight for his country were published and

British poet Rupert Brooke.
(Corbis Corporation. Reproduced by permission.)

became wildly popular in England. Brooke never saw action in the war; he was on his way to fight the Turks at Gallipoli when he contracted blood poisoning from an insect bite on his lip. He died on the island of Scyros in the Aegean Sea on April 23, 1915.

leges in the United States. Many British soldiers were therefore well-educated men who appreciated poetry.

British soldiers had a special relationship with literature. British schooling was based on the idea that understanding the poetry of the past makes people good citizens. Thus, all British students were familiar with a wide range of poets, from ancient Greek poets to those more recent, such as British writer Thomas Hardy. Many soldiers carried with them to the front a standard volume called the *Oxford Book of English Verse*, a collection of important poetry; others had recent publications of poetry sent to them. Such books were extremely popular at the front, for they provided a diversion from the horror and tedium of war. Fussell quotes the story of Herbert Read, who was mailed a copy of a book of verse by poet Robert Browning: "At first I was mocked in the dugout as a high-brow for reading *The Ring and the Book,* but saying nothing I waited until one of the scoffers idly picked it up. In ten minutes he was absorbed, and in three days we were fighting for turns to read it, and talking of nothing else at meals."

Schooled in poetry, many British soldiers turned to writing poetry to record their reactions to the war. And as it turned out, World War I produced more poetry than any war before or since. Hundreds of volumes of war poetry were published; according to John Lehmann, author of *The English Poets of the First World War,* "There was a period, during and directly after the War, when almost any young man who could express his thoughts and feelings in verse could find a publisher and a public." Poets—including Rupert Brooke, Siegfried Sassoon, Wilfred Owen, Edmund Blunden, Alan Seeger (the rare American), Robert Graves, Isaac Rosenberg, and many others—recorded all the various ways that soldiers experienced the war, from the first longings for glory to the final sickening confrontation with death. Many of these poems are now forgotten, but many others—such as the ones included below—are still remembered and taught. These poems provide a fascinating view of the first modern war.

 Alan Seeger (1888–1916)

The only major American war poet, Alan Seeger was born in New York City in 1888. Seeger attended Harvard College, where he dabbled in poetry and began to develop a reputation as a freethinker (someone who does not follow the conventions of his peers). After graduation he returned to New York City, but he grew to dislike life in America; he felt that Americans were uncivilized and incapable of enjoying life's true pleasures, such as fine wine, good food, and art. In 1912 Seeger moved to Paris, France.

When World War I began, Seeger leaped at the chance to enlist in the French Foreign Legion, a division of the French army that accepted enlistments from foreigners. Seeger hoped to find in war the intensity and excitement that he craved. Seeger served in the foreign legion for nearly two years, seeing action in battles at Aisne and Champagne, but he was bored whenever he was out of battle. He soothed his boredom in part by writing poems; his only collection of poetry was published in 1916. On July 4, 1916, Seeger took part in one of the major battles of the war, the Battle of the Somme. Pushing forward on the first day of the attack, he was gunned down by German machine-gun fire, crawled into a shell hole, and died.

The poetry of World War I closely reflects the attitudes that many soldiers had toward the war. The first poems—including those by Brooke and Seeger—brim with the confidence of soldiers who believe that they are embarking on a glorious adventure. For the first year or two of the war, many poems spoke of honor, glory, and patriotism; they compared the duties of modern soldiers with those of warriors celebrated in the epic poems of the ancient Greeks. Yet the slowly dawning horror of the continuing war began to reshape war poetry, just as it reshaped the attitudes of everyone involved in the war. As the war wore on, poets such as Wilfred Owen and Siegfried Sassoon began to write bitter, cutting verses about the horror of war and the failure of patriotic visions. After 1916, writes Lehmann, "the dreams were shattered, and patriotism became a matter of grim endurance against all odds, of despairing hope almost buried beneath the huge weight of disillusionment, of the need not to be defeated existing beside the belief that it was increasingly not merely stupid but almost criminal not to negotiate an end to the slaughter."

Things to remember while reading the poems of hope and glory by Rupert Brooke and Alan Seeger:

- The poems by Rupert Brooke and Alan Seeger hint at the attitudes poets had toward the war during the first period of war poetry, the period of hope and honor and glory. In these poems the poets speak of leaving the petty pleasures of civilian life for the exalted life of a soldier; they are romantic and hopeful.

- Literature and warfare went hand in hand during World War I. Many of the war poets composed their poems while sitting in the trenches waiting for a battle to begin; novelists and essayists also composed their works under the most difficult conditions. Reading was a common way of passing long hours between battles.

- Poetry can be difficult. Poets use uncommon and sometimes old-fashioned words to convey their ideas; they often refer to ancient myths or to other poems that most people today do not know. Poets condense meaning into tight knots of words, and it can be difficult to untie those knots. But the very things that make poetry difficult also make it rewarding. It may help to read the poems several times or to read them aloud. Think of a poem as a puzzle and see if you can solve it.

"I. Peace"
By Rupert Brooke

Now, God be thanked **Who has matched us with His hour,**
  And caught our youth, and wakened us from
    sleeping,
With hand made sure, clear eye, and sharpened power,
  To turn, as swimmers into cleanness leaping,
Glad from a world grown old and cold and weary,
  Leave the sick hearts that honour could not move,
And half-men, and their dirty songs and dreary,
  And all the little emptiness of love!

Oh! we, who have known shame, we have found
  release there,
  Where there's no ill, no grief, but sleep has mending,
  Naught broken **save** this body, lost but breath;
Nothing to shake the laughing heart's long peace there
  But only agony, and that has ending;
  And the worst friend and enemy is but Death.

"III. The Dead"
By Rupert Brooke

Blow out, you bugles, over the rich Dead!
  There's none of these so lonely and poor of old,
  But, dying, has made us rarer gifts than gold.
These laid the world away; poured out the red
Sweet wine of youth; gave up the years to be
  Of work and joy, and that unhoped serene,
  That men call age; and those who would have been,
Their sons, they gave, their immortality.

Who has matched us with His hour: Who has allowed us to be here at this important moment in history.

Naught: Nothing.

Save: Except.

*Blow, bugles, blow! They brought us, for our **dearth**,*
*   Holiness, lacked so long, and Love, and Pain.*
Honour has come back, as a king, to earth,
*   And paid his subjects with a royal wage;*
And nobleness walks in our ways again;
*   And we have come into our heritage.*

"I Have a Rendezvous with Death"

By Alan Seeger

*I have a **rendezvous** with Death*
At some disputed barricade,
When Spring comes back with rustling shade
And apple-blossoms fill the air—
I have a rendezvous with Death
When Spring brings back blue days and fair.

It may be he shall take my hand
And lead me into his dark land
And close my eyes and quench my breath—
It may be I shall pass him still.
I have a rendezvous with Death
On some scarred slope of battered hill,
When Spring comes round again this year
And the first meadow-flowers appear.

God knows 'twere better to be deep
Pillowed in silk and scented down,
Where Love throbs out in blissful sleep,
*Pulse **nigh** to pulse, and breath to breath*
Where hushed awakenings are dear. . .
But I've a rendezvous with Death
At midnight in some flaming town,
When Spring trips north again this year,
And I to my pledged word am true,
I shall not fail that rendezvous.

"Sonnet X"

By Alan Seeger

I have sought Happiness, but it has been
*A lovely rainbow, **baffling all pursuit**,*

Dearth: Shortage of, lack.

Rendezvous: A prearranged meeting.

Nigh: Near.

Baffling all pursuit: Always out of reach.

And tasted Pleasure, but it was a fruit
More fair of outward hue than sweet within.
*Renouncing both, **a flake in the ferment***
Of battling hosts that conquer or recoil,
*There only, **chastened** by fatigue and toil,*
I knew what came the nearest to content.
For there at least my troubled flesh was free
From the gadfly Desire that plagued it so;
Discord and Strife were what I used to know,
Heartaches, deception, murderous jealousy;
By War transported far from all of these,
Amid the clash of arms I was at peace.

"Sonnet XI: On Returning to the Front After Leave"

By Alan Seeger

***Apart** sweet women (for whom Heaven be blessed),*
Comrades, you cannot think how thin and blue
Look the leftovers of mankind that rest,
Now that the cream has been skimmed off in you.
War has its horrors, but has this of good—
That its sure processes sort out and bind
Brave hearts in one intrepid brotherhood
And leave the shams and imbeciles behind.
Now turn we joyful to the great attacks,
Not only that we face in a fair field
Our valiant foe and all his deadly tools,
But also that we turn disdainful backs
On that poor world we scorn yet die to shield—
That world of cowards, hypocrites, and fools.

A flake in the ferment / Of battling hosts that conquer or recoil: As an individual soldier caught in a clash between great nations, the poet is comparing himself to a flake—perhaps of snow—caught in a ferment, or storm.

Chastened: Subdued or worn out.

Apart: Apart from; other than.

Things to remember while reading the poems of disillusionment by Wilfred Owen and Siegfried Sassoon:

- The following five poems by Wilfred Owen and Siegfried Sassoon take a very different view of war. These are poems of harsh disillusionment. The authors seem to realize that there is no higher calling to war but merely a bitter struggle to survive.

- Though the romantic and optimistic poems of Alan Seeger and Rupert Brooke were very popular early in the war, the work of Owen and Sassoon was much more popular late in the war and afterwards. The change reflected in these poems is said to mark the emergence of modern literature, which focuses more on the perceptions of common people than earlier literature does.

Wilfred Owen.
(The Granger Collection. Reproduced by permission.)

"Strange Meeting"
By Wilfred Owen

It seemed that out of battle I escaped
Down some profound dull tunnel, long since scooped
Through granites which titanic wars had **groined.**

Yet also there encumbered sleepers groaned,
Too fast in thought or death to be bestirred.
Then, as I probed them, one sprang up, and stared
With piteous recognition in fixed eyes,
Lifting distressful hands, as if to bless.
And by his smile, I knew that sullen hall,—
By his dead smile I knew we stood in Hell.

With a thousand pains **that vision's face was grained;**
Yet no blood reached there from the upper ground,
And no guns thumped, or down the **flues** *made moan.*
'Strange friend,' I said, 'here is no cause to mourn.'
'None,' said that other, 'save the undone years,
The hopelessness. Whatever hope is yours,

Groined: Opened holes in.

That vision's face was grained: The man's face was etched with pain.

Flues: Chimneys of the tunnel.

Wilfred Owen (1893–1918)

Unlike poets Alan Seeger and Rupert Brooke, Wilfred Owen wrote not of the glory of war but of the pity of war. Owen was born in Oswestry, England, on March 18, 1893, to a humble, religious family. Owen excelled at school and eventually attended the University of London, but he was forced to leave the university when he ran short of money. He worked for a time as a reverend's assistant and as a schoolteacher, but he had not yet found his calling when he decided to enroll in the English army in the summer of 1915.

Owen served as an officer in the Second Battalion Manchester Regiment, and he saw plenty of action. Leading a regiment in a battle at Serre, he saw many of his men killed and wounded. These memories of battle would soon fuel an outpouring of poetry. In 1917 Owen was hospitalized with a concussion and shell shock (a term indicating that a soldier was so mentally distraught from fighting that he could no longer serve). At the Craiglockhart War Hospital in Edinburgh, Scotland, Owen met poet Siegfried Sassoon. The two poets spurred each other on, and both created some of their greatest works while at the hospital.

Owen returned to active duty in September 1918 and was soon sent to attack some of the Germans' strongest defensive positions on the Hindenburg line (a line of concrete-reinforced trenches built by the Germans). Owen earned a Military Cross (war medal) for his efforts, but he was soon killed in a battle on November 4, 1918, one week before the end of the war. Owen's friends and admirers—including Sassoon—made sure that Owen's poetry was published, and Owen is now considered one of the greatest of the war poets.

Was my life also; I went hunting wild
After the wildest beauty in the world,
Which lies not calm in eyes, or braided hair,
But mocks the steady running of the hour,
And if it grieves, grieves richlier than here.
For by my glee might many men have laughed,
And of my weeping something had been left,
Which must die now. I mean the truth untold,
The pity of war, the pity war distilled.
Now men will go content with what we spoiled,
Or, discontent, boil bloody, and be spilled.
They will be swift with swiftness of the tigress.

None will break ranks, though nations trek from progress.
Courage was mine, and I had mystery,
Wisdom was mine, and I had mastery:
To miss the march of this retreating world
Into vain **citadels** that are not walled.
Then, when much blood had clogged their chariot-wheels,
I would go up and wash them from sweet wells,
Even with truths that lie too deep for **taint**.
I would have poured my spirit **without stint**
But not through wounds; not on the **cess** of war.
Foreheads of men have bled where no wounds were.

I am the enemy you killed, my friend.
I knew you in this dark: for so you frowned
Yesterday through me as you jabbed and killed.
I parried; but my hands were loath and cold.
Let us sleep now. . . .'

"They"

By Siegfried Sassoon

The Bishop tells us: 'When the boys come back
They will not be the same; for they'll have fought
In a just cause: they lead the last attack
On Anti-Christ; their comrades' blood has bought
New right to breed an honourable race,
They have challenged Death and dared him face to face.'

'We're none of us the same!' the boys reply.
'For George lost both his legs; and Bill's stone blind;
Poor Jim's shot through the lungs and like to die;
And Bert's **gone syphilitic**: you'll not find
A chap who's served that hasn't found some change.'
And the Bishop said: 'The ways of God are strange!'

"Anthem for Doomed Youth"

By Wilfred Owen

What **passing-bells** for these who die as cattle?
—Only the monstrous anger of the guns.

Citadels: Fortresses.

Taint: Any trace of discredit or dishonor.

Without stint: Without limit.

Cess: Cessation, or end.

Gone syphilitic: Caught a venereal disease.

Passing-bells: Bells rung to announce a death.

Only the stuttering rifles' rapid rattle
*Can **patter out their hasty orisons.***
No mockeries now for them; no prayers nor bells;
*   Nor any voice of mourning save the choirs, —*
The shrill, demented choirs of wailing shells;
*   And bugles calling for them from sad **shires.***

What candles may be held to speed them all?
*   Not in the hands of boys but in their eyes*
Shall shine the holy glimmers of goodbyes.
*   The **pallor** of girls' brows shall be their **pall**;*
Their flowers the tenderness of patient minds,
And each slow dusk a drawing-down of blinds.

"Counter-Attack"

By Siegfried Sassoon

We'd gained our first objective hours before
While dawn broke like a face with blinking eyes,
***Pallid**, unshaved and thirsty, blind with smoke.*
Things seemed all right at first. We held their line,
*With bombers **posted**, Lewis guns well placed,*
And clink of shovels deepening the shallow trench.
*   The place was rotten with dead; green clumsy legs*
*   High-booted, sprawled and **grovelled** along the **saps**;*
*   And trunks, face downward in the sucking mud,*
*   Wallowed like trodden sand-bags loosely filled;*
*   And naked sodden buttocks, mats of hair,*
*   Bulged, clotted heads, slept in the plastering slime.*
*   And then the rain began—the jolly old rain!*

A yawning soldier knelt against the bank,
*Staring across the morning **blear** with fog;*
*He wondered when the **Allemands** would get busy;*
*And then, of course, they started with **five-nines***
Traversing, sure as fate, and never a dud.
Mute in the clamour of shells he watched them burst
Spouting dark earth and wire with gusts from hell,
*While **posturing giants** dissolved in drifts of smoke.*
He crouched and flinched, dizzy with galloping fear,
Sick for escape—loathing the strangled horror
And butchered, frantic gestures of the dead.

Patter out their hasty orisons: Speak their funeral prayers.

Shires: English country villages.

Pallor: Paleness.

Pall: Coffin.

Pallid: Lacking color or liveliness.

Posted: In position.

Grovelled: Crawled.

Saps: Covered trenches.

Blear: Blurred, dimmed.

Allemands: Germans.

Five-nines: Explosive shells.

Posturing giants: The poet is probably referring to the towers of smoke and dust that rise from shell blasts and are blown apart by the wind.

An officer came blundering down the trench:
'Stand-to and man the **fire-step!**' On he went. . .
Gasping and bawling, 'Fire-step . . . counter-attack!'
 Then the haze lifted. Bombing on the right
 Down the old sap: machine-guns on the left;
 And stumbling figures looming out in front.
 'O Christ, they're coming at us!' Bullets spat,
And he remembered his rifle . . . rapid fire . . .
And started blazing wildly . . . then a bang
Crumpled and spun him sideways, knocked him out
To grunt and wriggle: none heeded him; he choked
And fought the flapping veils of smothering gloom,
Lost in a blurred confusion of yells and groans. . .
Down, and down, and down, he sank and drowned,
Bleeding to death. The counter-attack had failed.

"Dulce Et Decorum Est"

By Wilfred Owen

Bent double, like old beggars under sacks,
Knock-kneed, coughing like hags, we cursed through
 sludge,
Till on the haunting flares **we turned our backs**
And towards our distant rest began to trudge.
Men marched asleep. Many had lost their boots
But limped on, **blood-shod**. All went lame, all blind;
Drunk with fatigue; deaf even to the hoots
Of tired, outstripped **Five-Nines** that dropped behind.

Gas! GAS! Quick, boys!—An ecstasy of fumbling,
Fitting the **clumsy helmets** just in time;
But someone still was yelling out and stumbling,
And flound'ring like a man in fire or lime. . . .
Dim, through the **misty panes and thick green light**,
As under a green sea, I saw him drowning.

In all my dreams, before my helpless sight,
He plunges at me, **guttering**, choking, drowning.

If in some smothering dreams you too could pace
Behind the wagon that we flung him in,
And watch the white eyes writhing in his face,

Fire-step: The top step of a trench.

Knock-kneed: Literally, an inward curvature of the legs, but here the poet is referring to legs bowed by the weight of a load.

We turned our backs: Retreated.

Blood-shod: Wearing blood for shoes; soldiers often lost their boots and were forced to march barefoot, cutting their feet.

Five-Nines: Explosive shells.

Clumsy helmets: Gas masks.

Misty panes and thick green light: The poet is referring to the experience of looking through the thick, foggy lenses of gas masks into the green fog of poison gas.

Guttering: In a sorry or degraded state.

British troops blinded by mustard gas in a German gas attack at Bethune, France, April 1918.

(Archive Photos. Reproduced by permission.)

His hanging face, like a devil's sick of sin;
If you could hear, at every jolt, the blood
*Come gargling from the **froth-corrupted lungs**,*
*Obscene as cancer, bitter as the **cud***
Of vile, incurable sores on innocent tongues,—
My friend, you would not tell with such high zest
To children ardent for some desperate glory,
*The old Lie: **Dulce et decorum est***
Pro patria mori.

What happened next . . .

For many of the poets who fought in World War I there
was no next. Rupert Brooke, Alan Seeger, and Wilfred Owen all
died in the war, ending their brief careers as poets. Others
spent the rest of their lives reliving and recounting their war
experiences. Poetry, of course, went on, but it was changed forever by the war. The war killed millions of men, but it also
killed off the kind of poetry that could urge men to die for
honor and glory and love of country. Future poets would never
again uncritically accept the romantic notions of warfare that
existed before World War I. The great poetic works that came
out after the war—especially T. S. Eliot's *The Waste Land* and
Ezra Pound's *Cantos*—all shared the ironic attitude displayed
by Owen and Sassoon. (Irony is the use of words and images to
convey something different from their literal meaning. For
example, these poets often used beautiful poetic language to
describe the demeaning effects of war.) Postwar literature of all
sorts is filled with images of people who are alienated from
grand ideas, lied to by bureaucracies, and who retreat into a
shell of self-protection. The war novels of Erich Maria Remarque and Ernest Hemingway share in this sense of alienation
and disillusionment (see the following excerpts from these
novelists).

Siegfried Sassoon (1886–1967)

One of the most significant of the war poets, Siegfried Sassoon was also one of the few who survived the war. Sassoon was born on September 8, 1886, to a family steeped in the literary and artistic culture of late nineteenth-century England. He acquired a gentleman's education and pursued the interests of a wealthy Englishman: poetry and foxhunting. His first collections of poetry, published between 1906 and 1916, were considered bland and uninteresting. But his activities in World War I soon shook this refined gentleman to his core and brought vitality to his writing.

Siegfried Sassoon. *(Corbis Corporation. Reproduced by permission.)*

Sassoon served as an officer in the Royal Welch Fusiliers, a British army regiment, and quickly earned a Military Cross (war medal) for valor in battle. But Sassoon saw more clearly than others the horror of war and the futility (hopelessness) of sending men into battles that meant certain slaughter. He published his first collection of war poems, titled *The Old Huntsman,* in 1917. Soon after, he wrote a letter condemning the British army leadership. He could have been court-martialed (prosecuted) for the letter, but he was instead diagnosed with shell shock (a term indicating that a soldier was so mentally distraught from fighting that he could no longer serve) and sent to the Craiglockhart War Hospital in Edinburgh, Scotland. At the hospital, Sassoon met fellow poet Wilfred Owen; the two poets encouraged each other and wrote some of their best poems in the hospital. Sassoon's poems address the horror and futility of war with a directness and an intensity rare in war poetry.

Sassoon survived the war and went on to create other works of real distinction. His trilogy of autobiographical novels, *Memoirs of George Sherston,* is considered one of the best accounts of the war. Sassoon also became actively engaged in politics, especially antiwar politics. He died on September 1, 1967.

Did you know . . .

- Of the four poets represented here, three died in the war: Alan Seeger, Wilfred Owen, and Rupert Brooke. Does knowing this change the way you understand their poetry?

- Wilfred Owen was killed just a week before the war ended. Literary scholars believe that he was one of the greatest of the war poets.

- Alan Seeger fought not with the American army but rather with the French foreign legion, a select fighting force made up of volunteers from all over the world.

For More Information

Books

Brooke, Rupert. *Rupert Brooke: The Collected Poems.* London: Sidgwick and Jackson, 1987.

Fussell, Paul. *The Great War and Modern Memory.* London and New York: Oxford University Press, 1975.

Lehmann, John. *The English Poets of the First World War.* London: Thames and Hudson, 1981.

Owen, Wilfred. *War Poems and Others.* Edited by Dominic Hibberd. London: Chatto and Windus, 1973.

Roberts, David, ed. *Minds at War: The Poetry and Experience of the First World War.* London: Saxon Books, 1996.

Roberts, David, ed. *Out in the Dark: Poetry of the First World War in Context and with Basic Notes.* London: Saxon Books, 1998.

Sassoon, Siegfried. *Collected Poems.* New York: Viking Press, 1949.

Seeger, Alan. *Poems.* New York: Charles Scribner's Sons, 1916.

Silkin, Jon, ed. *Penguin Book of First World War Poetry.* 2d ed. New York: Penguin, 1997.

Williams, Merryn. *Wilfred Owen.* Mid Clamorgan, United Kingdom: Seren Books, 1993.

Web sites

Introduction to First World War Poetry. [Online] http://info.ox.ac.uk/jtap/tutorials/intro (accessed January 2001).

"World War I." *Internet Modern History Sourcebook.* [Online] http://www.fordham.edu/halsall/mod/modsbook38.html (accessed January 2001).

Erich Maria Remarque

Excerpts from All Quiet on the Western Front
Translated by A. W. Wheen
Published in 1929

"We are not youth any longer," writes German novelist Erich Maria Remarque (1898–1970). "We don't want to take the world by storm. We are fleeing. We fly from ourselves. From our life. We were eighteen and had begun to love life and the world; and we had to shoot it to pieces. The first bomb, the first explosion, burst in our hearts. We are cut off from activity, from striving, from progress. We believe in such things no longer, we believe in war." When these sentiments, and others like them, appeared in a popular German magazine in 1928, they shocked and thrilled the German reading public; World War I was presented not in the patriotic tones used by politicians but in the weary, resigned words of the common man. In 1929 Remarque (pronounced Ruh-MARK) published his story as *Im Westen nichts Neues*, a novel better known by its English title, *All Quiet on the Western Front*. The novel became an immediate international success. It was rapidly acclaimed as the greatest war novel of all time, it was made into a popular Hollywood film, and it made an international celebrity of its author.

"To me the front is a mysterious whirlpool. Though I am in still water far away from its centre, I feel the whirl of the vortex sucking me slowly, irresistibly, inescapably into itself."

From All Quiet on the Western Front

German author Erich Maria Remarque, right, meets with German American film studio president Carl Laemmle. Remarque's novel, *All Quiet on the Western Front,* was made into a movie and won an Academy Award for Best Picture in 1930. *(Archive Photos. Reproduced by permission.)*

All Quiet on the Western Front consists of a series of loosely linked chapters narrated by Paul Bäumer, a young man just out of school who has volunteered to serve in the German army in World War I. Bäumer has joined the army with twenty of his schoolmates; by the time the novel begins, only four of them are still alive. Remarque explores the young soldiers' attitudes toward the war, their experiences in a hospital for the wounded behind the front, and Paul's disastrous visit home to comfort his dying mother. Most dramatically, Remarque details the young men's experiences in battle and their growing sense that the best they can hope for is to survive. In the end, however, not one of the young soldiers survives the war. Even Bäumer is killed in a short epilogue (a section at the end of a book that details what happens to the characters after the main story); he dies a month before the war ends, on a day when all was quiet on the Western Front.

The following excerpts present some of the key moments from the novel. In the first, Bäumer explains the ideals that motivated him and his friends to volunteer for service in the army. In the second and third excerpts, Bäumer describes how being at the battlefront changes the soldiers' attitudes; at the front there is no glory, only the quest for survival. In the next excerpt, Bäumer finds himself stranded in no-man's-land (the strip of land between opposing armies' trenches); there he stabs a French soldier whom he must then sit beside while the soldier dies. Firing a gun at the enemy from a distance made killing soldiers less personal. But this incident brings Bäumer face-to-face with his own responsibility for killing. In the final excerpt, Bäumer matter-of-factly relates the retreat of the German army.

Though these excerpts provide only a brief glimpse into the novel, they offer enough material for thinking about some of the issues that Remarque's novel raises. For example, how do Bäumer's attitudes toward the war change over time? Is war as glorious as he and his classmates believed when they volunteered to serve? What does Bäumer think about the role of the soldier in war? Compare Remarque's attitudes with those of American author Ernest Hemingway (see entry), whose war novel *A Farewell to Arms* also contemplates the role of the individual in wartime.

Things to remember while reading the excerpts from *All Quiet on the Western Front*:

- Remarque offers very detailed and realistic descriptions, but he never mentions specific battles. Critics have suggested that this was an effort to show that the feelings he describes are relevant to all battles.

- Another great war novel published in the late 1920s was Ernest Hemingway's *A Farewell to Arms*. While both novels are critical of the war, their authors propose different solutions to the perils of modern war. Hemingway suggests that the only way a man can survive the brutality of modern warfare is to protect himself and his personal values; Remarque holds out the hope that the men of different nations will recognize their common bond and refuse to go to war at the request of political leaders.

Erich Maria Remarque (1898–1970)

German novelist Erich Maria Remarque's reputation rests almost entirely on one novel, *All Quiet on the Western Front,* a depiction of two years of World War I service seen through the eyes of a German private. Remarque based the novel on his personal experiences in the war. Like the novel's narrator, Remarque served in the German army as a youth of eighteen; many of the characters in the novel are based on his school friends who served alongside him. However, *All Quiet on the Western Front* is not autobiography; most of the novel is fiction.

The author was born Erich Paul Remark on June 22, 1898, in the village of Osnabrück in Lower Saxony, Germany. His relatively poor family moved frequently during his youth, but he was an intelligent boy who did well at school. During high school he took courses to prepare him to

be a teacher, and it was from high school, in 1916, that he was drafted to serve in World War I. Remarque never saw action at the front, but he was injured slightly when a British shell exploded behind the lines. He spent most of the war recovering from his wounds in a hospital and was sent back into service just days before the war ended. Following the war, Remarque often appeared with war medals on his fancy clothes (he loved to dress well); many of his acquaintances questioned whether he had earned the medals.

Remarque taught school for a time after the war, but he was not happy in this profession. He held a series of jobs before becoming a writer with the magazine *Sport im Bild* in 1925. It was while working at the magazine that he wrote *All Quiet on the Western Front.* The novel was written in just six weeks. Remarque insisted that it was his

All Quiet on the Western Front

Excerpt from Chapter 2

Once it was different. When we went to the district commandant to enlist, we were a class of twenty young men, many of whom proudly shaved for the first time before going to the barracks. We had no definite plans for our future. Our thoughts of a career and occupation were as yet of too unpractical a character to furnish any first novel, though in truth he had written a novel in 1920 called *Die Traumbude*. Remarque was so ashamed of this first effort that he changed the spelling of his last name to avoid connection with the novel. The great, immediate success of *All Quiet on the Western Front* changed Remarque's life dramatically: He earned enough money to indulge his love of fine clothes and fast cars, but the opposition to his novel by German Nazis forced him to leave his country in 1931. Remarque settled first in Switzerland and then in the United States.

After the publication of *All Quiet on the Western Front*, Remarque was a celebrity. When he moved to the United States in 1938, he quickly became a major figure in Hollywood; he married film star Paulette Goddard (1911–1990) and was linked romantically to screen idols Marlene Dietrich (c. 1901–1992) and Greta Garbo (1905–1990). He also befriended American novelists F. Scott Fitzgerald (1896–1940) and Ernest Hemingway (1899–1961). Remarque was considered one of the most handsome and dashing men in Hollywood, and he even appeared in a film made from one of his novels.

Remarque continued to publish novels, many of which had themes similar to those in his most famous book, but none reached the popularity of *All Quiet on the Western Front*. Remarque never again felt welcome in his native Germany and his work—while esteemed throughout the world—is not so highly thought of in his own country, not only because he was so critical of German leaders and common people but also because his book shaped the way the rest of the world saw Germany. Remarque died in a hospital in Locarno, Switzerland, on September 25, 1970.

*scheme of life. We were still crammed full of vague ideas which gave to life, and to the war also an ideal and almost romantic character. We were trained in the army for ten weeks and in this time more profoundly influenced than by ten years at school. We learned that **a bright button is weightier than four volumes of Schopenhauer**. At first astonished, then embittered, and finally indifferent, we recognized that what matters is not the mind but the boot brush, not intelligence but the system, not freedom but drill. We became soldiers with eagerness and enthusiasm, but they have done everything to knock that out of us. After three weeks it was no longer incomprehensible to us that a **braided** postman should have more authority over us than had formerly our parents, our teachers, and the whole gamut of cul-*

A bright button is weightier than four volumes of Schopenhauer: Remarque is referring to the importance placed on a proper uniform in the military; he is complaining that, in the military, how one looks is more important than what one knows. Arthur Schopenhauer (1788–1860) was a German philosopher.

*ture from **Plato to Goethe**. With our young, awakened eyes we saw that the classical conception of the Fatherland held by our teachers resolved itself here into a renunciation of personality such as one would not ask of the **meanest** servants—salutes, springing to attention, parade-marches, presenting arms, right wheel, left wheel, clicking the heels, insults, and a thousand **pettifogging** details. We had fancied our task would be different, only to find we were to be trained for heroism as though we were circus-ponies. But we soon accustomed ourselves to it. We learned in fact that some of these things were necessary, but the rest merely show. Soldiers have a fine nose for such distinctions.* [Remarque, pp. 21–22]

All Quiet on the Western Front
Excerpt from Chapter 4

Our faces are neither paler nor more flushed than usual; they are not more tense nor more flabby—and yet they are changed. We feel that in our blood a contact has shot home. That is no figure of speech; it is fact. It is the front, the consciousness of the front, that makes this contact. The moment that the first shells whistle over and the air is rent with the explosions there is suddenly in our veins, in our hands, in our eyes a tense waiting, a watching, a heightening alertness, a strange sharpening of the senses. The body with one bound is in full readiness.

It often seems to me as though it were the vibrating, shuddering air that with a noiseless leap springs upon us; or as though the front itself emitted an electric current which awakened unknown nerve-centres. . . .

To me the front is a mysterious whirlpool. Though I am in still water far away from its centre, I feel the whirl of the vortex sucking me slowly, irresistibly, inescapably into itself.

From the earth, from the air, sustaining forces pour into us— mostly from the earth. To no man does the earth mean so much as to the soldier. When he presses himself down upon her long and powerfully, when he buries his face and his limbs deep in her from the fear of death by shell-fire, then she is his only friend, his brother, his mother; he stifles his terror and his cries in her silence and her security; she shelters him and releases him for ten seconds to live, to run, ten seconds of life; receives him again and often for ever.

Braided: Refers to the postman's uniform.

Plato to Goethe:
Philosophers typically studied in school; Greek philosopher Plato (c. 428–348 B.C.) and German philosopher and poet Johann Wolfgang von Goethe (1749–1832).

Meanest: Lowliest, poorest.

Pettifogging: Insignificant.

Earth!—Earth!—Earth!

Earth with thy folds, and hollows, and holes, into which a man may fling himself and crouch down. In the spasm of terror, under the hailing of annihilation, in the bellowing death of the explosions, O Earth, thou grantest us the great resisting surge of new-won life. Our being, almost utterly carried away by the fury of the storm, streams back through our hands from thee, and we, thy redeemed ones, bury ourselves in thee, and through the long minutes in a mute agony of hope bite into thee with our lips!

At the sound of the first droning of the shells we rush back, in one part of our being, a thousand years. By the animal instinct that it awakened in us we are led and protected. It is not conscious; it is far quicker, much more sure, less fallible, than consciousness. One cannot explain it. A man is walking along without thought or heed;—suddenly he throws himself down on the ground and a storm of fragments flies harmlessly over him;—yet he cannot remember either to have heard the shell coming or to have thought of flinging himself

A young German soldier stands in a deep trench at the beginning of combat in 1915. *(Archive Photos. Reproduced by permission.)*

down. But had he not abandoned himself to the impulse he would now be a heap of mangled flesh. It is this other, this second sight in us, that has thrown us to the ground and saved us, without our knowing how. If it were not so, there would not be one man alive from Flanders to the Vosges.

We march up, moody or good-tempered soldiers—we reach the zone where the front begins and become on the instant human animals. [Remarque, pp. 54–56]

All Quiet on the Western Front

Excerpt from Chapter 6

The front is a cage in which we must await fearfully whatever may happen. We lie under the network of arching shells and live in a suspense of uncertainty. Over us, Chance hovers. If a shot comes, we can duck, that is all; we neither know nor can determine where it will fall.

It is this Chance that makes us indifferent. A few months ago I was sitting in a dug-out playing **skat**; after a while I stood up and went to visit some friends in another dug-out. On my return nothing more was to be seen of the first one, it had been blown to pieces by a direct hit. I went back to the second and arrived just in time to lend a hand digging it out. In the interval it had been buried.

It is just as much a matter of chance that I am still alive as that I might have been hit. In a bomb-proof dug-out I may be smashed to atoms and in the open may survive ten hours' bombardment unscathed. No soldier outlives a thousand chances. But every soldier believes in Chance and trusts his luck. [Remarque, p. 101]

All Quiet on the Western Front

Excerpt from Chapter 9

[Paul has gone forward in an attack, but the attack has stopped and most of the other Germans have retreated. Paul is stranded out in no-man's-land, the open ground between the opposing armies, huddling in a shell hole. He lies down, hoping that any enemy soldiers who see him will think he is already dead.]

Skat: A card game for three players.

The crash of the shells bursts in my ears. If our fellows make a counter-raid I will be saved. I press my head against the earth and listen to the muffled thunder, like the explosions of quarrying—and raise it again to listen for the sounds on top.

The machine-guns rattle. I know our barbed wire entanglements are strong and almost undamaged;—parts of them are charged with a powerful electric current. The rifle fire increases. They have not broken through; they have to retreat.

I sink down again, huddled, strained to the uttermost. The banging, creeping, the clanging becomes audible. One single cry yelling amongst it all. They are raked with fire, the attack is repulsed.

Already it has become somewhat lighter. Steps hasten over me. The first. Gone. Again, another. The rattle of machine-guns becomes an unbroken chain. Just as I am about to turn round a little, something heavy stumbles, and with a crash a body falls over me into the shell-hole, slips down, and lies across me—

*I do not think at all, I make no decisions—**I strike madly at home**, and feel only how the body suddenly convulses, then becomes limp, and collapses. When I recover myself, my hand is sticky and wet.*

The man gurgles. It sounds to me as though he bellows, every gasping breath is like a cry, a thunder—but it is not only my heart pounding. I want to stop his mouth, stuff it with earth, stab him again, he must be quiet, he is betraying me; now at last I regain control of myself, but have suddenly become so feeble that I cannot any more lift my hand against him.

So I crawl away to the farthest corner and stay there, my eyes glued on him, my hand grasping the knife—ready, if he stirs, to spring at him again. But he won't do so any more, I can hear that already in his gurgling.

I can see him indistinctly. I have but one desire, to get away. If it is not soon it will be too light; it will be difficult enough now. Then as I try to raise up my head I see it is impossible already. The machine-gunfire so sweeps the ground that I should be shot through and through before I could make one jump. . . .

[Paul huddles in the hole with the wounded French soldier. Time passes, though how much is not clear.]

It is early morning, clear and grey. The gurgling continues, I stop my ears, but soon take my fingers away again, because then I cannot hear the other sounds [of battle].

I strike madly at home: He strikes wildly at the soldier who has fallen into the hole; earlier Paul had decided that he must kill anyone he faces.

Scene from the 1930 film *All Quiet on the Western Front,* depicting Paul huddled in a shell hole with the wounded French soldier. *(The Kobal Collection. Reproduced by permission.)*

The figure opposite me moves. I shrink together and involuntarily look at it. Then my eyes remain glued to it. A man with a small pointed beard lies there; his head is fallen to one side, one arm is half-bent, his head rests helplessly upon it. The other hand lies on his chest, it is bloody.

He is dead, I say to myself, he must be dead, he doesn't feel anything any more; it is only the body that is gurgling there. Then the head tries to raise itself, for a moment the groaning becomes louder, his forehead sinks back upon his arm. The man is not dead, he is dying, but he is not dead. I drag myself toward him, hesitate, support myself on my hands, creep a bit farther, wait, again a terrible journey. At last I am beside him.

Then he opens his eyes. He must have heard me, for he gazes at me with a look of utter terror. The body lies still, but in the eyes there is such an extraordinary expression of fright that for a moment I think they have power enough to carry the body off with them. Hundreds of miles away with one bound. The body is still perfectly still, without *a sound, the gurgle has ceased, but the eyes cry out, yell, all the life is gathered together in them for one tremendous effort to flee, gathered together there in a dreadful terror of death, of me.*

My legs give way and I drop to my elbows. "No, no," I whisper.

The eyes follow me. I am powerless to move so long as they are there. . . .

[Paul reaches out to the man and sees that he is thirsty.]

His mouth stands half open, it tries to form words. The lips are dry. My water bottle is not there. I have not brought it with me. But there is water in the mud, down at the bottom of the crater. I climb down, take out my handkerchief, spread it out, push it under and scoop up the yellow water that stains through into the hollow of my hand.

He gulps it down. I fetch some more. Then I unbutton his tunic in order to bandage him if it is possible. In any case I must do it, so that if the fellows over there capture me they will see that I wanted to help him, and so will not shoot me. He tries to resist, but his hand is too feeble. The shirt is stuck and will not come away, it is buttoned at the back. So there is nothing for it but to cut it open.

I look for the knife and find it again. But when I begin to cut the shirt the eyes open once more and the cry is in them again and the demented expression, so that I must close them, press them shut and whisper: "I want to help you, Comrade, camerade, camerade, camerade—" eagerly repeating the word, to make him understand.

There are three stabs. My field dressing covers them, the blood runs out under it, I press it tighter; there; he groans.

That is all I can do. Now we must wait, wait.

These hours. . . . The gurgling starts again—but how slowly a man dies! For this I know—he cannot be saved, I have, indeed, tried to tell myself that he will be, but at noon this pretence breaks down and melts before his groans. If only I had not lost my revolver crawling about, I would shoot him. Stab him I cannot.

By noon I am groping on the outer limits of reason. Hunger devours me, I could almost weep for something to eat, I cannot struggle against it. Again and again I fetch water for the dying man and drink some myself.

This is the first time I have killed with my hand, whom I can see close at hand, whose death is my doing. **Kat and Kropp and Müller**

Kat and Kropp and Müller:
Paul's friends in the army.

have experienced it already, when they have hit someone; it happens to many, in hand-to-hand fighting especially—

But every gasp lays my heart bare. This dying man has time with him, he has an invisible dagger with which he stabs me: Time and my thoughts. . . .

In the afternoon, about three, he is dead. . ..

[Trapped in the crater with the dead man, Paul nearly goes mad. Soon he speaks to the dead man.]

The silence spreads. I talk and must talk. So I speak to him and to say to him: "Comrade, I did not want to kill you. If you jumped in here again, I would not do it, if you would be sensible too. But you were only an idea to me before, an abstraction that lived in my mind and called forth its appropriate response. It was that abstraction I stabbed. But now, for the first time, I see you are a man like me. I thought of your hand-grenades, of your bayonet, of your rifle; now I see your wife and your face and our fellowship. Forgive me, comrade. We always see it too late. Why do they never tell us that you are poor devils like us, that your mothers are just as anxious as ours, and that we have the same fear of death, and the same dying and the same agony—Forgive me, comrade; how could you be my enemy? If we threw away these rifles and this uniform you could be my brother just like Kat and Albert. Take twenty years of my life, comrade, and stand up—take more, for I do not know what I can even attempt to do with it now." [Remarque, pp. 215–21, 223]

[Paul grieves for the dead man, promises the man that he will not kill again, opens the man's wallet and sees photographs of the man's family. Then Paul's friends rescue him and tell him that he only did what he had to do.]

All Quiet on the Western Front
Excerpt from Chapter 11

Our lines are falling back. There are too many fresh English and American regiments over there. There's too much corned beef and white wheaten bread. Too many new guns. Too many aeroplanes.

*But we are emaciated and starved. Our food is bad and mixed up with so much substitute stuff that it makes us ill. The factory owners in Germany have grown wealthy;—**dysentery** dissolves our bowels. The **latrine poles** are always densely crowded; the people at home*

Dysentery: An intestinal disease accompanied by high fever and severe diarrhea.

Latrine poles: Long poles on which soldiers would sit while relieving themselves into a trench dug in the ground.

ought to be shown these grey, yellow, miserable, wasted faces here, these bent figures from whose bodies the colic wrings out the blood, and who with lips trembling and distorted with pain, grin at one another and say:

"It is not much sense pulling up one's trousers again—"

*Our artillery is fired out, it has too few shells and the barrels are so worn that they shoot uncertainly, and scatter so widely as even to fall on ourselves. We have too few horses. Our fresh troops are anaemic boys in need of rest, who cannot carry a pack, but merely know how to die. By thousands. They understand nothing about warfare, they simply go on and let themselves be shot down. A **single flyer routed two companies** of them for a joke, just as they came fresh from the train—before they had ever heard of such a thing as cover.* [Remarque, pp. 280–81]

Single flyer routed two companies: An enemy pilot flew over and shot two groups of soldiers.

What happened next . . .

Remarque's war novel had enormous impact when it was published. Many readers loved the novel's realistic, unsentimental view of the alternating monotony and terror of wartime; others appreciated the book's depiction of the wide gulf between civilians and those who served in the war. Pacifists (people opposed to war on principle) praised the book as a powerful antiwar statement. *All Quiet on the Western Front* sold more than a million copies in Germany in its first year of publication, and millions more when the translated version appeared in England, France, and the United States. It was made into a film in 1930 and won the Academy Award for Best Picture and Best Director. Not surprisingly, *All Quiet on the Western Front* also brought its author great fame and wealth.

While Remarque was a hero to many for so clearly depicting the futility (hopelessness) of war, he also angered many within Germany. Some said that his novel was not literature and that he had merely given the public what it wanted. Others accused him of outright treachery (betrayal) toward his nation. Such critics said that the novel made light of the great sacrifices made by German soldiers and citizens; these critics felt that the book was intended "to sap the energies of the German nation at a time when it [had] to assert itself in the face of a hostile world if it [was] to survive," according to Christine R. Barker and R. W. Last, authors of *Erich Maria Remarque*. The National Socialist German Workers' (Nazi) Party was openly opposed to the book, citing as heresy (a belief that goes against official policy) Remarque's suggestion that German soldiers did not believe fully in fighting for the glory of the nation. The Nazis burned Remarque's book and protested the showing of the film in Germany. (Nazi opposition to the book only made it more attractive to citizens who feared the rise of the Nazi Party.)

The violent opposition to his book soon forced Remarque to flee Germany. It also raised the status of the book greatly, for now both the novel and its author stood as a living protest to the warlike tendencies of the modern state. Remarque lived first in Switzerland and later settled in the United States. He wrote more novels, several of which are considered quite good, but none quite so famous as his first.

Did you know . . .

- Though Remarque served in World War I, he never saw action on the front lines. His accounts of battle are products of his imagination, though they have been praised for their accuracy.

- The film version of *All Quiet on the Western Front* was one of the first movies to use sound; previous movies had been silent. The film proved to many critics that sound could help make a movie better.

- *All Quiet on the Western Front* is the first in a trilogy of books Remarque wrote about World War I. The other two books are *The Road Back* (1931) and *The Three Comrades* (1937).

For More Information

Books

Barker, Christine R., and R. W. Last. *Erich Maria Remarque*. London: Oswald Wolff, 1979.

Holmes, Richard. *The Western Front*. New York: TV Books, 2000.

Hoobler, Dorothy, and Thomas Hoobler. *The Trenches: Fighting on the Western Front in World War I*. New York: Putnam, 1978.

Remarque, Erich Maria. *All Quiet on the Western Front*. Trans. A. W. Wheen. 1929. New York: Fawcett Crest, 1987.

Ernest Hemingway

Excerpt from A Farewell to Arms
Published in 1929

Ernest Hemingway's *A Farewell to Arms* is a famous war novel that came out just a year after Erich Maria Remarque's *All Quiet on the Western Front* was published in Germany. Like Remarque, Hemingway had direct experience of the war; the book depicts the moral desolation of war from an American's point of view. Hemingway's novel provides some excellent descriptions of the horrors of warfare on the Italian front. John Keegan, historian and author of *The First World War,* calls Hemingway's description of the Italian retreat in late 1917 "one of the greatest literary evocations of military disaster." Hemingway strips the language of glory and patriotism away from the war and presents it as a cruel, dehumanizing. The following excerpts showcase both of these elements of Hemingway's novel; the lean, spare writing style for which Hemingway became famous is evident throughout.

Still in high school when the United States entered World War I on April 6, 1917, aspiring writer Ernest Hemingway wanted to join the bands of patriots volunteering for service. But poor eyesight and his parents' reluctance to have him serve kept him from joining the war effort. By 1918, however,

"We stood in the rain and were taken out one at a time to be questioned and shot. So far they had shot every one they had questioned."

From A Farewell to Arms

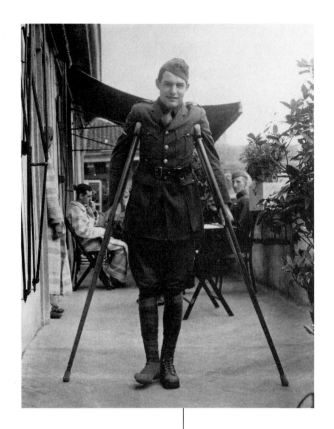

Ernest Hemingway, at a hospital in Milan, Italy, in 1918, recovers from injuries sustained during the war.
(Corbis Corporation. Reproduced by permission.)

Hemingway had found another way to place himself at the center of the world's most dramatic event: He volunteered for duty as an ambulance driver for the Red Cross. Hemingway arrived in Paris, France, in May 1918 and was quickly sent to the Italian front. He soon found himself near the battles between the Italians and the Austrians, with the assignment of bringing injured Italian soldiers back from the front in an aging Fiat ambulance. Hemingway was delivering supplies to soldiers near Fossalta di Piave on July 8, 1918, when an Austrian shell exploded nearby. Hemingway helped some wounded soldiers get to safety, but he was soon felled by fragments of shrapnel and Austrian machine-gun bullets. He was awarded the Italian Silver Medal of Military Valour and sent to a hospital in Milan. Hemingway was the second American to be wounded in Italy, and he was celebrated as a hero in the American newspapers.

At the Italian hospital, Hemingway fell in love with a nurse named Agnes von Kurowsky, the model for *Farewell*'s Catherine Barkley. He also befriended several Italian soldiers, who told him many stories of their wartime exploits. By the time Hemingway recovered from his injuries, the war was over, and he returned home to Chicago. For the next decade he committed himself to one goal: becoming the world's greatest writer. Shortly after the war, Hemingway returned to Paris, where he perfected his art under the guidance of writers Gertrude Stein (1874–1946) and Ezra Pound (1885–1972). Hemingway's first collection of stories, *In Our Time* (1925), was widely praised, and his first novel, *The Sun Also Rises* (1926), was greeted by great critical acclaim. By 1927 he had begun working on a novel based on his experiences as an ambulance driver in World War I.

Hemingway finished the first draft of *A Farewell to Arms* in 1928 and completed revisions by January 1929. The

novel tells the story of an American ambulance driver, Frederic Henry, who is injured while serving on the Italian front. Henry is sent to a Milan hospital, where he falls in love with a nurse, Catherine Barkley. Henry returns to the front just in time to take part in the massive Italian retreat from a German and Austrian advance. Scrambling with several friends to escape the German advance, Henry is captured by Italian soldiers who are executing officers who have deserted their troops. Diving into a river, Henry deserts the army, finds Catherine Barkley, and escapes with her to neutral Switzerland. Henry believes that he can make a "separate peace" with Catherine far from the chaos of the war, but this peace is shattered when Catherine dies shortly after giving birth to a stillborn child.

Scribner's Magazine bought serial rights to *A Farewell to Arms* (which meant they would publish it in chapters over a number of months) for sixteen thousand dollars, and the book was published whole in September 1929. It quickly became a best-seller. Some critics felt that the novel was sentimental for

Ambulance drivers load stretchers onto American Red Cross ambulances on the Italian front. Not eligible for military service himself, Ernest Hemingway volunteered for duty as an ambulance driver for the Red Cross. *(Corbis Corporation. Reproduced by permission.)*

its portrayal of the romance between Frederic Henry and Catherine Barkley, but most were impressed by the novel's bleak and tragic view of the world. Henry's ideas of the nobility and glory of war are rudely destroyed by his experience of combat, and his retreat into the safe haven of his relationship with Catherine is also destroyed by forces beyond his control. Hemingway had an existential view of the world (the view that the individual is solely responsible for his or her actions in a hostile or indifferent world), one that saw man absolutely alone and without solace in a world that could easily crush him. It was a modern attitude, created by the war that shook the world. *A Farewell to Arms* established Hemingway as one of the world's greatest living writers and exerted a huge influence on other American writing. It also shaped the way succeeding generations thought about World War I.

Things to remember while reading the excerpts from *A Farewell to Arms*:

- *A Farewell to Arms* is based partly on Hemingway's own experiences, but it is not autobiographical. Hemingway did not join in the Italian retreat from the advancing German and Austrian armies, and he did not desert and escape to Switzerland. He used his imagination and the stories he heard from Italian soldiers to construct the world of the novel. Though the book is fiction, historians and soldiers have praised the accuracy of Hemingway's presentation of the war.

- One of Hemingway's most distinctive techniques as an author was to leave things out of his writing. He believed that if he told the story well enough, the reader could sense those things that he did not mention. Can you find places in the excerpts where this might be true? How do Hemingway and the Italian soldiers feel about the carabinieri (battle police), for example?

- The Italian army was notorious for the harshness of its discipline. Soldiers who did not follow orders were routinely executed, and officers were often quite scornful of the men under their command.

- The following excerpts come from the beginning, middle, and end of the novel, which is narrated by Frederic Henry.

How does Henry's attitude about life and war change as the novel progresses? What do you think has caused the change in his thinking?

A Farewell to Arms

Excerpt from Chapter 9

[On the night before an attack, Frederic Henry talks with several Italian mechanics about the coming battle. Henry is an officer—a lieutenant, or "Tenente"—and the mechanics do not want to speak freely around him at first. They are discussing which soldiers will go to battle and how they will fight.]

"Who goes to the attack?" asked Gavuzzi.

*"**Bersaglieri.**"*

"All bersaglieri?"

"I think so."

"There aren't enough troops here for a real attack."

"It is probably to draw attention from where the real attack will be."

"Do the men know that who attack?"

"I don't think so."

"Of course they don't," Manera said. "They wouldn't attack if they did."

"Yes, they would," Passini said. "Bersaglieri are fools."

"They are brave and have good discipline," [Henry] said.

"They are big through the chest by measurement, and healthy. But they are still fools."

*"The **granatieri** are tall," Manera said. This was a joke. They all laughed.*

*"Were you there, **Tenente**, when they wouldn't attack and they shot every tenth man?"*

"No."

Bersaglieri: Members of an elite group of shock troops who will lead the attack.

Granatieri: Grenadiers, or grenade throwers.

Tenente: Lieutenant.

"It is true. They lined them up afterward and took every tenth man. **Carabinieri** shot them."

"Carabinieri," said Passini and spat on the floor. "But those grenadiers; all over six feet. They wouldn't attack."

"If everybody would not attack the war would be over," Manera said.

"It wasn't that way with the granatieri. They were afraid. The officers all came from such good families."

"Some of the officers went alone."

"A sergeant shot two officers who would not get out."

"Some troops went out."

"Those that went out were not lined up when they took the tenth men."

"One of those shot by the carabinieri is from my town," Passini said. "He was a big smart tall boy to be in the granatieri. Always in Rome. Always with the girls. Always with the carabinieri." He laughed. "Now they have a guard outside his house with a bayonet and nobody can come to see his mother and father and sisters and his father loses his civil rights and cannot even vote. They are all without law to protect them. Anybody can take their property."

"If it wasn't that that happens to their families nobody would go to the attack."

"Yes. **Alpini** would. . . . Some bersaglieri."

"Bersaglieri have run too. Now they try to forget it."

"You should not let us talk this way, Tenente. **Evviva l'esercito**," Passini said sarcastically.

"I know how you talk," I said. "But as long as you drive the cars and behave—"

"—and don't talk so other officers can hear," Manera finished.

"I believe we should get the war over," I said. "It would not finish it if one side stopped fighting. It would only be worse if we stopped fighting."

"It could not be worse," Passini said respectfully. "There is nothing worse than war."

"Defeat is worse."

Carabinieri: Italian military police.

Alpini: Mountain soldiers.

Evviva l'esercito: Long live the army.

"I do not believe it," Passini said still respectfully. "What is defeat? You go home."

"They come after you. They take your home. They take your sisters."

"I don't believe it," Passini said. "They can't do that to everybody. Let everybody defend his home. Let them keep their sisters in the house."

"They hang you. They come and make you be a soldier again. Not in the auto-ambulance, in the infantry."

"They can't hang every one."

"An outside nation can't make you be a soldier," Manera said. "At the first battle you all run."

"Like the **Tchecos** ."

"I think you do not know anything about being conquered and so you think it is not bad."

"Tenente," Passini said. "We understand you let us talk. Listen. There is nothing as bad as war. We in the auto-ambulance cannot even realize at all how bad it is. When people realize how bad it is they cannot do anything to stop it because they go crazy. There are some people who never realize. There are people who are afraid of their officers. It is with them the war is made."

"I know it is bad but we must finish it."

"It doesn't finish. There is no finish to a war."

"Yes there is."

Passini shook his head.

"War is not won by victory. What if we take San Cabriele? What if we take the Carso and Monfalcone and Trieste? Where are we then? Did you see all the far mountains to-day? Do you think we could take all them too? Only if the Austrians stop fighting. One side must stop fighting. Why don't we stop fighting? If they come down into Italy they will get tired and go away. They have their own country. But no, instead there is a war."

"You're an **orator**."

"We think. We read. We are not peasants. We are mechanics. But even the peasants know better than to believe in a war. Everybody hates this war."

Tchecos: Literally "Czechs"; they seem to be referring to some Czech soldiers who ran away from battle.

Orator: Public speaker.

"There is a class that controls a country that is stupid and does not realize anything and never can. That is why we have this war."

"Also they make money out of it."

"Most of them don't," said Passini. "They are too stupid. They do it for nothing. For stupidity."

"We must shut up," said Manera. "We talk too much even for the Tenente."

"He likes it," said Passini. "We will convert him."

"But now we will shut up," Manera said.

"Do we eat yet, Tenente?" Gavuzzi asked.

"I will go and see," I said. Gordini stood up and went outside with me. . . . [Hemingway, pp. 49–51]

[Later in the same chapter Henry is injured when an Austrian trench mortar hits the building in which he and the mechanics are resting. In the injury scene, the narrator (Henry) relates his thoughts as they occur to him. This writing technique is called stream of consciousness.]

I ate the end of my piece of cheese and took a swallow of wine. Through the other noise I heard a cough, then came the chuh-chuh-chuh-chuh—then there was a flash, as when a blast-furnace door is swung open, and a roar that started white and went red and on and on in a rushing wind. I tried to breathe but my breath would not come and I felt myself rush bodily out of myself and out and out and out and all the time bodily in the wind. I went out swiftly, all of myself, and I knew I was dead and that it had all been a mistake to think you just died. Then I floated, and instead of going on I felt myself slide back. I breathed and I was back. The ground was torn up and in front of my head there was a splintered beam of wood. In the jolt of my head I heard somebody crying. I thought somebody was screaming. I tried to move but I could not move. I heard the machine-guns and rifles firing across the river and all along the river. There was a great splashing and I saw the star-shells go up and burst and float whitely and rockets going up and heard the bombs, all this in a moment, and then I heard close to me some one saying "Mama Mia! Oh, mama Mia!" I pulled and twisted and got my legs loose finally and turned around and touched him. It was Passini and when I touched him he screamed. His legs were toward me and I saw in the dark and the light that they were both smashed above the knee. One leg was gone and the other was held by tendons and part of the trouser and the stump twitched and jerked as though it were not connected. He bit his arm and moaned, "Oh mama mia, mama Mia," then, "Dio te salve, Maria. Dio te salve, Maria. Oh Jesus shoot me Christ shoot me mama mia mama Mia oh purest lovely Mary shoot me. Stop it. Stop it. Stop it. Oh Jesus lovely Mary stop it. Oh oh oh oh," then choking, "Mama mama mia." Then he was quiet, biting his arm, the stump of his leg twitching.

"*Porta feriti!*" I shouted holding my hands cupped. "*Porta feriti!*" I tried to get closer to Passini to try to put a tourniquet on the legs but I could not move. I tried again and my legs moved a little. I could pull backward along with my arms and elbows. Passini was quiet now. I sat beside him, undid my tunic and tried to rip the tail of my shirt. It would not rip and I bit the edge of the cloth to start it. Then I thought of his **puttees**. I had on wool stockings but Passini wore puttees. All the drivers wore puttees but Passini had only one leg. I unwound the puttee and while I was doing it I saw there was no need to try and make a tourniquet because he was dead already. I made sure he was dead. There were three others to locate. I sat up straight and as I did so something inside my head moved like the weights on a doll's eyes and it hit me inside in back of my eyeballs. My legs felt warm and wet and my shoes were wet and warm inside. I knew that I was hit and leaned over and put my hand on my knee. My knee wasn't there. My hand went in and my knee was down on my shin. I wiped my hand on my shirt and another floating light came very slowly down and I looked at my leg and was very afraid. Oh, God, I said, get me out of here. I knew, however, that there had been three others. There were four drivers. Passini was dead. That left three. Some one took hold of me under the arms and somebody else lifted my legs.

"There are three others," I said. "One is dead."

"It's Manera. We went for a stretcher but there wasn't any. How are you, Tenente?"

"Where is Gordini and Gavuzzi?"

"Gordini's at the post getting bandaged. Gavuzzi has your legs. Hold on to my neck, Tenente. Are you badly hit?"

"In the leg. How is Gordini?"

"He's all right. It was a big trench mortar shell."

"Passini's dead."

"Yes. He's dead."

Porta feriti: Open wound.

Puttees: Strips of cloth wound around the legs from the ankles to the knees for protection; these were part of the Italian uniform.

A shell fell close and they both dropped to the ground and dropped me. "I'm sorry, Tenente," said Manera. "Hang onto my neck."

"If you drop me again."

"It was because we were scared."

"Are you unwounded?"

"We are both wounded a little."

"Can Gordini drive?"

"I don't think so."

They dropped me once more before we reached the post.

"You sons of bitches," I said.

"I am sorry, Tenente," Manera said. "We won't drop you again."
[Hemingway, pp. 54–56]

[Henry is taken to a hospital for surgery. At the hospital where he is sent to recuperate, he is reunited with Catherine Barkley, an English nurse he had met earlier in the book. They fall in love but are separated when Henry's injuries heal and he returns to his ambulance unit at the front. In the following excerpt Henry has been talking with an ambulance driver named Gino about the coming Italian assault and the rumor that the Austrians are planning a major assault of their own. Henry's thoughts about Gino make up one of the best-known passages of the novel.]

A Farewell to Arms

Excerpt from Chapter 27

[Gino said. . . .] "We won't talk about losing. There is enough talk about losing. What has been done this summer cannot have been done in vain."

I did not say anything. I was always embarrassed by the words sacred, glorious, and sacrifice and the expression in vain. We had heard them, sometimes standing in the rain almost out of earshot, so that only the shouted words came through, and had read them, on proclamations that were slapped up by billposters over other proclamations, now for a long time, and I had seen nothing sacred, and the things that were glorious had no glory and the sacrifices were like the stockyards at Chicago if nothing was done with the meat except to

Italian troops fend off an attack from a trench carved into a mountainside.
(Archive Photos. Reproduced by permission.)

bury it. There were many words that you could not stand to hear and finally only the names of places had dignity. Certain numbers were the same way and certain dates and these with the names of the places were all you could say and have them mean anything. Abstract words such as glory, honor, courage, or hallow were obscene beside the concrete names of villages, the numbers of roads, the names of rivers, the numbers of regiments and the dates. Gino was a patriot, so he said things that separated us sometimes, but he was also a fine boy and I understood his being a patriot. He was born one. He left with Peduzzi in the car to go back to Gorizia.

It stormed all that day. The wind drove down the rain and everywhere there was standing water and mud. The plaster of the broken houses was gray and wet. Late in the afternoon the rain stopped and from our number two post I saw the bare wet autumn country with clouds over the tops of the hills and the straw screening over the roads wet and dripping. The sun came out once before it went down and shone on the bare woods beyond the ridge. There were many Austrian guns in the woods on that ridge but only a few fired. I watched the sudden round puffs of shrapnel smoke in the sky above a broken farmhouse near where the line was; soft puffs with a yellow white flash in the centre. You saw the flash, then heard the crack, then saw the smoke ball distort and thin in the wind. There were many iron shrapnel balls in the rubble of the houses and on the road beside the broken house where the post was, but they did not shell near the post that afternoon. . . .[Hemingway, p. 178]

A Farewell to Arms

Excerpt from Chapter 30

[The rumored Austrian assault becomes a reality, and the entire Italian army falls back in retreat. Henry and his ambulance corps are separated from the main body of troops and make their way south to the Tagliamento River on their own, losing several of their men along the way. As Henry and a man named Piani reach the river, it is clear that the military police are executing officers who they believe have left their units. Henry is also singled out for execution.]

*That was a very strange night. I do not know what I had expected, death perhaps and shooting in the dark and running, but nothing happened. We waited, lying flat beyond the ditch along the main road while a German battalion passed, then when they were gone we crossed the road and went on to the north. We were very close to Germans twice in the rain but they did not see us. We got past the town to the north without seeing any Italians, then after a while came on the main channels of the retreat and walked all night toward the Tagliamento. I had not realized how gigantic the retreat was. The whole country was moving, as well as the army. We walked all night, making better time than the vehicles. My leg ached and I was tired but we made good time. It seemed so silly for **Bonello** to have decided*

Bonello: One of the members of the ambulance team.

156   **World War I: Primary Sources**

*to be taken prisoner. There was no danger. We had walked through two armies without incident. If **Aymo** had not been killed there would never have seemed to be any danger. No one had bothered us when we were in plain sight along the railway. The killing came suddenly and unreasonably. I wondered where Bonello was. . . .*

[Henry and Piani approach a crowd of soldiers at a bridge over the river.]

"Here I am, Tenente," [said Piani, who was walking with Henry] . He was a little ahead in the jam. No one was talking. They were all try-ing to get across as soon as they could: thinking only of that. We were almost across. At the far end of the bridge there were officers and cara-binieri standing on both sides flashing lights. I saw them silhouetted against the skyline. As we came close to them I saw one of the officers point to a man in the column. A carabiniere went in after him and came out holding the man by the arm. He took him away from the road. We came almost opposite them. The officers were scrutinizing every one in the column, sometimes speaking to each other, going for-ward to flash a light in some one's face. They took some one else out just before we came opposite. I saw the man. He was a lieutenant-colonel. I saw the stars in the box on his sleeve as they flashed a light on him. His hair was gray and he was short and fat. The carabiniere pulled him in behind the line of officers. As we came opposite I saw one or two of them look at me. Then one pointed at me and spoke to a carabiniere. I saw the carabiniere start for me, come through the edge of the column toward me, then felt him take me by the collar. . . .

"What's the meaning of this?" I tried to shout but my voice was not very loud. They had me at the side of the road now.

"Shoot him if he resists," an officer said. "Take him over back."

"Who are you?"

"You'll find out."

"Who are you?"

"Battle police," another officer said.

*"Why don't you ask me to step over instead of having one of these **airplanes** grab me?"*

They did not answer. They did not have to answer. They were bat-tle police.

"Take him back there with the others," the first officer said. "You see. He speaks Italian with an accent."

"So do you, you —," I said.

Aymo: Another ambulance team member.

Airplanes: Slang for the carabinieri.

*"Take him back with the others," the first officer said. They took me down behind the line of officers below the road toward a group of people in a field by the river bank. As we walked toward them shots were fired. I saw flashes of the rifles and heard the **reports**. We came up to the group. There were four officers standing together, with a man in front of them with a carabiniere on each side of him. A group of men were standing guarded by carabinieri. Four other carabinieri stood near the questioning officers, leaning on their carbines. . . . I looked at the man the officers were questioning. He was the fat gray-haired little lieutenant-colonel they had taken out of the column. The questioners had all the efficiency, coldness and command of themselves of Italians who are firing and are not being fired on.*

"Your brigade?"

He told them.

"Regiment?"

He told them.

"Why are you not with your regiment?"

He told them.

"Do you not know that an officer should be with his troops?"

He did.

That was all. Another officer spoke.

"It is you and such as you that have let the barbarians onto the sacred soil of the fatherland."

"I beg your pardon," said the lieutenant-colonel.

"It is because of treachery such as yours that we have lost the fruits of victory."

"Have you ever been in a retreat?" the lieutenant-colonel asked.

"Italy should never retreat."

We stood there in the rain and listened to this. We were facing the officers and the prisoner stood in front and a little to one side of us.

"If you are going to shoot me," the lieutenant-colonel said, "please shoot me at once without further questioning. The questioning is stupid." He made the sign of the cross. The officers spoke together. One wrote something on a pad of paper.

"Abandoned his troops, ordered to be shot," he said.

Reports: Shots from the rifles.

*Two carabinieri took the lieutenant-colonel to the river bank. He walked in the rain, an old man with his hat off, a carabiniere on either side. I did not watch them shoot him but I heard the shots. They were questioning some one else. This officer too was separated from his troops. He was not allowed to make an explanation. He cried when they read the sentence from the pad of paper, and they were questioning another when they shot him. They made a point of being intent on questioning the next man while the man who had been questioned before was being shot. In this way there was obviously nothing they could do about it. I did not know whether I should wait to be questioned or make a break now. I was obviously **a German in Italian uniform.** I saw how their minds worked; if they had minds and if they worked. They were all young men and they were saving their country. The second army was being reformed beyond the Tagliamento. They were executing officers of the rank of major and above who were separated from their troops. They were also dealing summarily with German agitators in Italian uniform. . . . We stood in the rain and were taken out one at a time to be questioned and shot. So far they had shot every one they had questioned. The questioners had that beautiful detachment and devotion to stern justice of men dealing in death without being in any danger of it. They were questioning a full colonel of a line regiment. Three more officers had just been put in with us.*

"Where was his regiment?"

I looked at the carabinieri. They were looking at the new-comers. The others were looking at the colonel. I ducked down, pushed between two men, and ran for the river, my head down. I tripped at the edge and went in with a splash. The water was very cold and I stayed under as long as I could. I could feel the current swirl me and I stayed under until I thought I could never come up. The minute I came up I took a breath and went down again. It was easy to stay under with so much clothing and my boots. When I came up the second time I saw a piece of timber ahead of me and reached it and held on with one hand. I kept my head behind it and did not even look over it. I did not want to see the bank. There were shots when I ran and shots when I came up the first time. I heard them when I was almost above water. There were no shots now. The piece of timber swung in the current and I held it with one hand. I looked at the bank. It seemed to be going by very fast. There was much wood in the stream. The water was very cold. We passed the brush of an island above the water. I held onto the timber with both hands and let it take me along. The shore was out of sight now. [Hemingway, 208–9, 211–15]

A German in Italian uniform: Henry assumes the Italian soldiers will think he is a German spy and will shoot him.

A Farewell to Arms

Excerpt from Chapter 41

[After Henry deserts the army, he smuggles himself aboard a train to escape. He meets up with Catherine Barkley in the resort town of Stresa, on Lake Maggiore, and they soon flee the country in a row-boat, rowing to Switzerland on the north end of the lake. The couple decides to stay in Switzerland until Catherine gives birth to their baby. But in childbirth everything goes wrong: The baby is born dead, and Catherine is bleeding internally and likely to die. As Henry contemplates Catherine's likely death, he muses about the meaning of life.]

*Now Catherine would die. That was what you did. You died. You did not know what it was about. You never had time to learn. They threw you in and told you the rules and the first time they caught you off base they killed you. Or they killed you gratuitously like Aymo. Or gave you the syphilis like **Rinaldi**. But they killed you in the end. You could count on that. Stay around and they would kill you.*

Once in camp I put a log on top of the fire and it was full of ants. As it commenced to burn, the ants swarmed out and went first toward the centre where the fire was; then turned back and ran toward the end. When there were enough on the end they fell off into the fire. Some got out, their bodies burnt and flattened, and went off not knowing where they were going. But most of them went toward the fire and then back toward the end and swarmed on the cool end and finally fell off into the fire. I remember thinking at the time that it was the end of the world and a splendid chance to be a messiah and lift the log off the fire and throw it out where the ants could get off onto the ground. But I did not do anything but throw a tin cup of water on the log, so that I would have the cup empty to put whiskey in before I added water to it. I think the cup of water on the burning log only steamed the ants. [Hemingway, p. 310]

[*A Farewell to Arms* ends with Catherine Barkley's death. Frederic Henry leaves her body in the hospital and walks out into the cold Swiss rain to an uncertain future. He has deserted the Italian army to make a life with Catherine, and now she is gone.]

Rinaldi: A friend of Henry's.

What happened next . . .

Hemingway's war novel was both an immediate and a lasting success. It sold twenty-eight thousand copies in one month in the fall of 1929, and it made Hemingway an international celebrity. In *The American Novel from Cooper to Faulkner,* Carlos Baker writes that "Among the American novels which deal with the First World War of 1914–18, *A Farewell to Arms* has stood up under the weathering of the years as well as any and far better than most. . . . *Soldier's Pay* by William Faulkner and *Three Soldiers* by John Dos Passos have long since begun to show signs of literary senility. . . . [Hemingway's book] manages to remain singularly undated at the same time that it perfectly embodies the Zeitgeist [spirit of the age], the governing moral essence of that far-away time."

Hemingway went on to become one of the most acclaimed and popular American writers of the twentieth century. Hemingway loved danger: When he wasn't hunting for big game or boxing, he was serving as a war correspondent in conflicts across the globe. Hemingway turned his experiences during the Spanish civil war into another great novel, *For Whom the Bell Tolls* (1939). He won the Nobel Prize, the world's highest prize for literature, for his 1952 novel *The Old Man and the Sea.* As the years went on, however, the quality of Hemingway's writing declined. No one knew it better than he did. Depressed at his declining talent, Hemingway ended his life on July 2, 1961.

Did you know . . .

- Ernest Hemingway is now widely considered the master of the modern short story. His themes and techniques have been widely imitated or adopted by writers up to the present day.

- The Italian retreat that Hemingway depicts in *A Farewell to Arms* was modeled on the retreat from Caporetto that nearly destroyed the Italian army. Launching an aggressive surprise attack on October 24, 1917, the Germans and Austrians broke through the Italian lines and started a massive Italian retreat. The Central Powers drove the Italians back nearly seventy-five miles and captured 275,000 prisoners along the way. Many of the Italians simply gave up, for the

Italian army's will to fight had been all but extinguished by their constant, futile attacks. The Italians finally built defensive lines near the Piave River, north of Venice, which they maintained until the end of the war.

- Hemingway hoped to marry Agnes von Kurowsky, the nurse on whom he had based the character of Catherine Barkley. Kurowsky broke his heart when she ended their relationship by sending a letter from Europe.

For More Information

Books

Hemingway, Ernest. *A Farewell to Arms*. New York: Charles Scribner's Sons, Reprint 1957.

Keegan, John. *The First World War*. New York: Alfred A. Knopf, 1999.

Lyttle, Richard B. *Ernest Hemingway: The Life and the Legend*. New York: Atheneum, 1992.

Wiener, Gary, ed. *Readings on A Farewell to Arms*. San Diego, CA: Greenhaven Press, 2000.

Articles

Baker, Carlos. "Ernest Hemingway, *A Farewell to Arms*." In *The American Novel from Cooper to Faulkner,* ed. Wallace Stegner. New York: Basic Books, 1965.

Web sites

Berridge, H. R. "Ernest Hemingway's *A Farewell to Arms*." [Online] http://www.haxors.com/booknotes/Farewell.To.Arms.txt (accessed January 2000).

The Home Front

While soldiers fought on the battlefronts of World War I, civilians were also said to be fighting on a front of their own—the "home front." Every war requires support from the people left at home, but World War I required more home front support than earlier wars had. In previous conflicts, armies met on battlefields that were removed from civilian population centers, and noncombatants were rarely touched by the war unless a member of their family was killed. Wars were short and armies small. World War I was different.

Within months of the war's beginning in 1914, it became clear that World War I was a new kind of war. The heavy casualties and massive expenditures of matériel (war supplies) demanded a constant supply of fresh, able-bodied soldiers, manufactured weapons, equipment, and food. While thousands of men in Great Britain heeded the initial calls to serve their country voluntarily, huge numbers of men in other countries were conscripted into (required to join) their countries' armies. The governments of Great Britain, France, and Germany reordered their economies to support the war effort. Civilians were asked to perform new jobs and give up many of

As the war drew more and more men into military service, women in all combatant countries took on increased responsibilities in munitions factories, construction, and other essential industries.
(Archive Photos. Reproduced by permission.)

their conveniences in order to help the war effort; every member of society was mobilized in the single goal of defeating the enemy. In short, World War I brought "total war" to Great Britain, France, and Germany. Although not a "total war" in other countries, World War I stressed the economic life of citizens around the world.

The work of women, children, and men on the home front was important to the success of their armies on the battlefront. As millions of men took up arms, those on the home front organized to support them. Women stepped into jobs once held only by men. When France entered the war in 1914 at harvest time, farmers left for the war and their wives had to bring in the crops. Two years later in Great Britain, 400,000 women organized into a uniformed Women's Land Army to plow fields and complete other farmwork. With mounting casualties and a continual draw of civilian men into the army, women in all combatant countries took on more responsibilities in munitions factories, construction, and other essential industries. In Germany women working in the machine industry numbered 75,000 before the war and almost 500,000 by 1916, according to Neil M. Heyman in his book *World War I.*

In addition to performing manual labor, people on the home front were also asked to ration (give out in limited amounts) food, gas, coal, and clothing. In Germany and Russia, women had an especially difficult time during the war. Although they worked long hours in factories or on farms, women could not pay for or find enough food to eat or fuel to heat their homes. People would stand for hours in bread and coal lines, hoping that the supply would last until their turn came. Food was so scarce in Germany by the winter of 1915 that many regions were rationed to one half-pound loaf of bread per person daily. The ration was lowered in 1918, and other rationed supplies of potatoes, milk, and meat steadily declined as the war wore on. The lack of coal during the winters caused some women to fear that their children would freeze to death; few people could afford to heat private homes. Clothing in Germany was so scarce that people started wearing clothes made of paper and wooden shoes.

France and Britain suffered from inflation (rising prices) and had to use rationing in the last two years of the war, but their populations remained relatively healthy. In fact, they became very resourceful in creating new sources and kinds of food. When the price of meat in Great Britain rose 40 percent in the first year of the war, people heeded the government's calls to plant gardens for private consumption and to cut their consumption of meat. In fact, the "war bread" (bread made of a mixture of wheat and other food, mostly potatoes) available in Britain was more nutritious than the bread some Britons had consumed before the war, and poor families actually experienced higher standards of living. In the United States, food production increased by 25 percent during the war, but the government still asked everyone to conserve food by saving leftovers and having "Meatless Tuesdays" and "Porkless Thursdays."

In addition to the manual labor and daily sacrifices of their citizens, governments needed funding for the war effort. In the United States, for example, the war cost forty-four million dollars per day in 1918. To raise money, governments raised taxes and asked people to invest their personal savings in war bonds (guaranteed loans to the government). In the United States the sale of war bonds, called Liberty Loans, raised more than twenty-one billion dollars. Governments also needed raw material for industrial production. People were asked to donate their metal goods to be recycled for the manufacture of munitions and other equipment.

The war caused tremendous stress in people's lives. Many were torn between feelings of patriotism and a nagging worry that their government leaders didn't have the people's best interests at heart. As the realities of the war made life more and more difficult, people in all countries began to wonder if their sacrifices were worth the effort. Would their lives improve if their side won the war? If they stopped working, would they be able to force their governments to provide them with enough food to eat and enough coal to keep them from freezing?

Government leaders needed to persuade the masses to continue supporting the war. The most effective method of persuasion was propaganda (official information that provides selected truths, exaggerations, and sometimes outright lies to persuade people to a certain point of view). This chapter provides a sampling of various **propaganda posters** that governments used to enlist the help of men, women, and children on the home front. As the war continued, the messages changed: The first enthusiastic calls to service were replaced with more and more desperate and heavy-handed messages.

But government propaganda did not persuade everyone. **Rosa Luxemburg** (1870–1919) had spent most of her life trying to organize workers to revolt against what she thought were oppressive governments in Poland, Russia, and Germany. No amount of propaganda could change Luxemburg's determination to incite a workers' revolution. She did not see World War I as an opportunity for people to be patriotic, but rather as an impediment to the workers' revolution she so desired. Between 1915 and 1918 Luxemburg remained imprisoned in Germany for trying to start a revolt. But from prison she worked tirelessly, writing eloquent appeals to working-class people, asking them to recognize that the war was doing them no good and that their interests would be better served by a popular revolution that could overturn the government and stop the war. In an excerpt from her most famous appeal, entitled *The Junius Pamphlet,* Luxemburg describes how detrimental the war is to the lives of working-class people and encourages Germans to embrace **socialism** and overthrow the German government.

Cries of discontent like Luxemburg's worried governments, because the massive reorganization of industry required the support of every able-bodied person in every combatant country. Germany, Great Britain, and France completely reshaped their economies to produce goods for the war. But Russia was not able to make the adjustments necessary for a wartime economy. Plagued by labor disputes before the war, Russia buckled under the stress of having so many men leave for the Eastern Front. Though Russia managed to increase its industrial output to supply its army, it could not feed its population or offer enough fuel for heat. Russia dissolved into revolution by 1917 and became the first country to withdraw from the war. **Telegrams from two American consulates in Russia** at the time draw an interesting picture of the events that triggered the country's civil disorder.

Socialism: A social system in which the means of producing and distributing goods are owned collectively, and the benefits of production are distributed to all members of society.

World War I
Propaganda Posters

Examples of propaganda posters used during World War I to encourage citizens to support their countries' war efforts

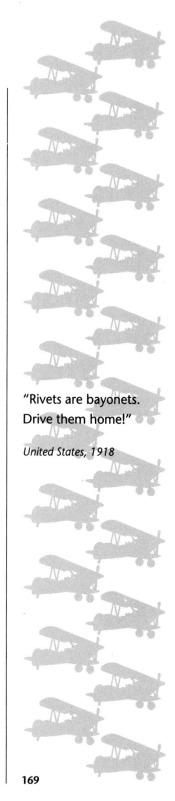

"Rivets are bayonets. Drive them home!"

United States, 1918

G overnments of all combatant countries realized that they would need the full support of their citizens to effectively wage war, and they set out to shape popular opinion in a variety of ways. Through propaganda—the spreading of ideas about the war that were favorable to the government—and censorship—the suppression of war news that was unfavorable to the government—governments tried to control how people viewed the war and the enemy. One of the main purposes of propaganda was to persuade people to act. Governments needed men to enlist, women to take on new jobs in factories and in hospitals, anyone with extra money to purchase war bonds (guaranteed loans made to the government), and everyone to conserve food and other daily necessities.

Governments used a variety of methods to spread propaganda. Newspapers were censored. In both France and Germany the newspapers were under the direct control of the military. War departments submitted their version of how the war was going, and newspaper editors were expected to print that news exactly as it was given to them. Even British newspapers, which had prided themselves on their independence, were

Albert Sterner was among the many artists commissioned to create war posters for their government. *(Corbis Corporation. Reproduced by permission.)*

forced to get most of their news from the government press bureau. They hesitated to publish news that was unfavorable to the government for fear that they would be prosecuted under the Defense of the Realm Act (DORA), which gave the government broad powers to limit free expression. The result of this direct and indirect control of the news was that people within the combatant countries rarely received accurate reports about the war. Victories were exaggerated, and defeats were downplayed. When French soldiers mutinied in the summer of 1917, news of the trouble never even reached French civilians. In the end, the lack of accurate news may have been the only thing that kept citizens in both France and Germany from rising up in revolt.

Government officials, religious groups, and civic organizations were asked to spread propaganda by word of mouth as well. Hatred of both France and Great Britain was encouraged by German officials and preached in churches. Special emphasis was placed on hating Great Britain, because Britain had blockaded German ports and was seen as the biggest obstacle to German victory. The German people were banned from speaking English; businesses and streets bearing English names received quick name changes to German. People throughout Germany sang a "Hymn of Hate" against England, which concluded "We love as one, we hate as one, we have one foe and one alone—ENGLAND," according to John Williams in *The Other Battleground*. The U.S. government asked youth groups like the Boy Scouts of America (see box on page 212) to spread the government-supplied "truth" about the war, urging such groups to talk with anyone who would listen.

Posters were one of the most important means of spreading propaganda during World War I. Before the age of television and radio, governments had fewer ways to communicate with the masses, so they invested heavily in the production of posters that grabbed citizens' attention. The following sampling of posters from different countries illustrates the various attempts to persuade people to support the war effort. At the beginning of the war, posters reflected optimism and enthusiasm and the expectation that victory would be quick and glorious. As the fighting continued with no end in sight, governments struggled to maintain public support. Posters shifted to desperate pleas for help, but they soon began to rely on hatred of the enemy as the central reason to support war efforts. While posters calling for men to enlist are the most familiar, others were designed specifically to encourage support on the home front. Several posters illustrated that teamwork among people on the home front and those on the battlefield would lead to victory. As the numbers of wounded rose, posters encouraged women to become nurses with the Red Cross. The general message was that everyone's work was needed.

Things to remember while reading World War I propaganda posters:

- Posters needed to persuade people who were suffering economic hardships to sacrifice even more for the war effort. Notice how the early posters are almost cheerful and the later ones are much more somber.

- Imagine yourself as a person in each country during the war. What would you do for the country's good?

- Why do you think the tone of the posters changed as the war progressed?

Enthusiastic posters from the beginning of World War I

Great Britain (1914): "Follow Me!"

A recruitment poster. Until 1916, when the draft was introduced, Great Britain was the only major European nation that relied on volunteers for its military forces.
(Hoover Institution Archives.)

Russia (1916):
Translation of title:
"Subscribe to the 5½%
war loan and pave the
way to victory."
(The Art Archive. Reproduced
by permission.)

France (1916):
Translation of title: "We'll get them! The 2nd National Defense Loan. Subscribe." A French soldier encourages his comrades to join the fight.

Created by Abel Faivre (1867–1945).
(Library of Congress.)

Desperate attempts to continue support for the war

United States (1917): "His Liberty Bond paid for in full."

The image of the fallen soldier is meant to entice passersby into giving more money to support the war.

Created by William Allen Rogers.
(Hoover Institution Archives.)

France (1918): Translation of title: "For the last quarter hour, help me! Subscriptions of the National Loan available at the Banque Nationale de Credit."

Pictures General Ferdinand Foch (1851–1929) overseeing his troops. In 1918, Foch was appointed commander-in-chief of the Allied forces.

Created by Sem (1863–1934).
(Library of Congress.)

Austria (1917):
Translation of title:
"And you?"

Created by Alfred Roller.
(Hoover Institution Archives.)

United States (c.1918): "Rivets are bayonets. Drive them home!"

This poster emphasizes the cooperation between U.S. soldiers at the front and the machinists back home producing war supplies.

Created by John E. Sheridan. *(Hoover Institution Archives.)*

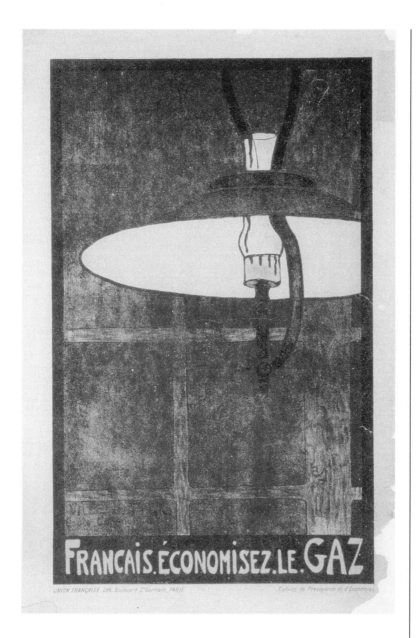

France (1918):
Translation of title:
"Frenchpeople, save gas."
(Library of Congress.)

Horror of the enemy

United States (1918): "Remember Belgium. Buy Bonds. Fourth Liberty Loan."

Depicts an evil German soldier dragging away an innocent young Belgian girl. *(National Archives. Reproduced by permission.)*

Great Britain (1918):
"To prevent this—buy War
Savings Certificates now."

This poster depicts German
soldiers mistreating slave
laborers in a factory. The
German spiked helmets, no
longer in use by 1918,
continued to be used on
posters as a strong
anti-German symbol.

Created by
F. Gregory Brown.
(Hoover Institution Archives.)

Women's help needed

The Greatest Mother in the World

United States (1918): "The greatest mother in the world."

A Red Cross nurse holds a wounded U.S. soldier.

Created by Alonzo Earl Foringer.
(Library of Congress.)

Great Britain (c.1915): "These women are doing their bit. Learn to make munitions."

Poster depicts a new member of the workforce starting her factory job as a soldier, in background, goes off to war. *(Corbis Corporation. Reproduced by permission.)*

THESE WOMEN ARE DOING THEIR BIT

LEARN TO MAKE MUNITIONS

Russia (1916):
Translation of title:
"Everything for the war."
(Corbis Corporation.
Reproduced by permission.)

France (1918):
Translation of title: "For the homeland, rest comrades."

This postcard depicts a nurse with bayonet watching guard over French soldiers while they rest.
(Archive Photos. Reproduced by permission.)

POUR LA PATRIE

Reposez, Camarades!...

What happened next . . .

Although most countries were ready to begin a conventional war in 1914, none were prepared for the extreme sacrifices that World War I demanded. Every economy struggled with the burden of the massive war effort. The ability of individual countries to increase their production of both war supplies and food made the difference between winning and losing the war, according to historian Paul Kennedy in *The Rise and Fall of the Great Powers*. Victory would ultimately go to the countries that balanced their need to build guns with their need to feed people.

As a group, combatant countries increased their munitions production from 4 percent of national income before the war to about 25 to 33 percent during the war, according to Kennedy. In the first two years of the war, Russia increased its production of both food and munitions impressively, but did not have adequate roads or railway systems to distribute the goods along its massive battlefront. Germany did not balance its productive capacity well either. It poured all its energy and resources into munitions production and neglected its farming industry. Kennedy quotes a German scholar who noted that "by concentrating lopsidedly on producing munitions, the military managers of the German economy thus brought the country to the verge of starvation by the end of 1918." The Allied powers succeeded in balancing industrial and agricultural production the best, and they received a huge boost when the United States entered the war in 1917. The United States brought impressive production power to the Allies. According to Kennedy, the United States could, by itself, produce two and a half times the industrial output of Germany; America also produced half of the world's supply of food exports at the time.

Women's Suffrage

The need for increased factory output in the combatant countries during World War I placed more women than ever in industrial jobs, which had traditionally been held by men. Women's rights groups in Great Britain and the United States supported their calls for women's **suffrage** by citing women's role in the war effort. The women's rights movement had come close to securing the vote for women just before the war broke out; by war's end, women's valuable war contributions on the homefront fully justified women's suffrage. Although men displaced women in farm and factory jobs after the war, the importance of women's wartime role in the labor force was recognized. In 1921 women in the United States were granted the right to vote; in 1928 Great Britain's women also achieved that right.

Suffrage: The right to vote.

Did you know . . .

- Women in Germany were encouraged to save their combed-out hair for use in drive belts and insulation.

- Germans were asked to contribute their household items made of aluminum, copper, brass, nickel, and zinc to be recycled for use by the army.

- In France some skilled workers were conscripted, or forced, to return from the trenches on the battlefield to work in munitions factories.

- Women and veterans worked in the factories of every nation during the war; in Germany even children supported the war effort with their labor.

For More Information

Books

Dolan, Edward F. *America in World War I*. Brookfield, CT: Millbrook Press, 1996.

Heyman, Neil M. *World War I*. Westport, CT: Greenwood Press, 1997.

Kennedy, Paul. *The Rise and Fall of the Great Powers*. New York: Random House, 1987.

Paret, Peter, Beth Irwin Lewis, and Paul Paret. *Persuasive Images: Posters of War and Revolution*. Princeton, NJ: Princeton University Press, 1992.

Williams, John. *The Other Battleground: The Home Fronts: Britain, France and Germany, 1914–1918*. Chicago: Henry Regnery, 1972.

Winter, J. M. *The Experience of World War I*. New York: Oxford University Press, 1989.

Winter, Jay, and Blaine Baggett. *The Great War and the Shaping of the 20th Century*. New York: Penguin Studio, 1996.

Web sites

"The First World War: The Home Front." [Online] http://www.sackville.wsussex.sch.uk/FWWhome.htm (accessed February 2001).

"The Great War and the Shaping of the 20th Century." [Online] http://www.pbs.org/greatwar (accessed February 2001).

Rosa Luxemburg

The Junius Pamphlet

Written April 1915
Originally published in Zurich, Switzerland,
February 1916, and illegally distributed in Germany.
Translated from *Politische Schriften* by Dave Hollis and
reprinted from the Marxists.org Internet Archive, available online
at http://www.marxists.org/archive/luxembur/index.htm.

Millions of men and women supported the war and worked diligently for victory, but others vehemently objected to the conflict. Rosa Luxemburg spent her life trying to incite workers to rise up and overthrow their governments. Imprisoned several times for trying to start a revolution, Luxemburg never lost her convictions and was eventually killed for them. Luxemburg's is a dramatic case of what can happen when a person disagrees with the dominant form of government.

In Germany, Luxemburg became one of the most vocal and influential speakers against the war. She is remembered as one of the most eloquent speakers for socialism, a political/economic belief that workers should own property, manage production, and govern themselves collectively. Born Rozalia Luksenburg in Poland in 1870, Luxemburg became active in the socialist movement before graduating from high school at age seventeen. By age nineteen, Luxemburg had become such a strong and active influence in the Polish socialist movement that she had to leave Russian-occupied Poland to avoid arrest. She went into exile in Zurich, Switzerland, where she began studies at the University of Zurich.

"One thing is certain. The world war is a turning point. It is foolish and mad to imagine that we need only survive the war, like a rabbit waiting out the storm under a bush, in order to fall happily back into the old routine once it is over. The world war. . .has changed us."

Rosa Luxemburg

Rosa Luxemburg was one of the most vocal and influential speakers against the war. *(Archive Photos. Reproduced by permission.)*

In Zurich, Luxemburg began collaborating with Leo Jogiches (1867–1919), a wealthy political activist with whom she would have a longtime political alliance and love affair. In 1892, Luxemburg and Jogiches created the Social Democracy for the Kingdom of Poland (SDKP), a Marxist political party (a party that followed the thinking of Karl Marx [1818–1883] and advocated class struggle and revolution). Luxemburg and Jogiches started rallying supporters with the party's newspaper, *Sprawa Robotwicza* ("Worker's Cause"). Luxemburg continued to advocate for common workers to take a more active part in government and to be able to own and manage property collectively. Luxemburg embraced Marxism, believing that capitalism would eventually fail when workers rose up to claim their rights. Over the next ten years, Luxemburg devoted herself to the fair treatment of workers and worked tirelessly to promote the SDKP in Poland and Germany. By 1901, Luxemburg had become a leader in the social democratic parties in both of these countries. She was a charismatic speaker and traveled extensively to support her cause. In 1903, Luxemburg represented Poland and Germany at the International Socialist Bureau Congress; she was the only woman present. The essay she presented, "Social Reform or Revolution," established the goals of the congress.

On January 22, 1905, Russian soldiers and cavalrymen massacred Russian workers who had been peacefully striking. In response to this incident, Luxemburg tried to incite a workers' revolution through her speeches and political writings in Russian-occupied Poland. The massacre, called Bloody Sunday, provoked widespread strikes and uprisings throughout Russian territory that lasted until December. For her part in the uprisings, Luxemburg was imprisoned by Russian authorities in Poland, but she continued to conduct her activism from jail by writing letters and pamphlets.

World War I dashed Luxemburg's hopes for a workers' revolution. For years Luxemburg had tried to unite workers against nationalist war efforts. She had thought that Germany's Social Democratic party believed as she did. When the party gave its support to the war in 1914, Luxemburg was infuriated. She was outspoken in her criticism of the German government and the war. As a result, she spent from 1915 to 1918 in jail for public disobedience. From prison, Luxemburg continued her efforts to bring about a workers' revolution: She wrote letters and pamphlets that her supporters smuggled out to the public. In 1915, she wrote one of her most famous pamphlets, *The Junius Pamphlet*. This piece lays the foundation of the Spartacus League, a group she founded with others to overthrow the German government. In the pamphlet she discusses the impact of World War I on the working class and explains why the working class should embrace socialism.

Things to remember while reading the *Junius Pamphlet*:

- The *Junius Pamphlet* was originally a document titled "The Crisis of the Social Democracy" signed "Junius."

- In the *Junius Pamphlet,* Luxemburg criticizes the socialist political party, the Social Democratic Party of Germany (SPD), for ignoring workers' interests in favor of **imperialist** ones. The SPD was a huge political force in Germany. The party could reach thousands of its supporters through its 39 daily papers, 28 bi-weeklies, and nine weekly papers.

- Even though Luxemburg was angry with the SPD, she did not want Marxists to be divided and worked to keep the differences of opinion from keeping them from uniting for a revolution.

- Luxemburg thought war was an obstacle for the revolution, but she thought bloodshed was necessary for the revolution.

The Junius Pamphlet

Excerpt from Chapter 1

*The scene has changed fundamentally [since the war began]. The **six weeks' march to Paris** has grown into a world drama. Mass slaughter has become the tiresome and monotonous business of the day and the end is no closer. . . .*

Gone is the euphoria. Gone the patriotic noise in the streets, . . . the swaying crowds in the coffee shops with ear-deafening patriotic songs surging ever higher, whole city neighborhoods transformed into mobs ready to denounce, to mistreat women, to shout hurrah and to induce delirium in themselves by means of wild rumors. . . .

*The spectacle is over. . . . The trains full of **reservists** are no longer accompanied by virgins fainting from pure jubilation. They no longer greet the people from the windows of the train with joyous smiles. Carrying their packs, they quietly trot along the streets where the public goes about its daily business with **aggrieved visages**.*

Imperialist: A government's efforts to increase power by capturing new territories or nations.

Six weeks' march to Paris: Refers to the Schlieffen plan, the Germans' strategy to win the war on the Western Front in six weeks' time.

Reservists: Enlisted soldiers.

Aggrieved visages: Distressed faces.

*In the **prosaic** atmosphere of pale day there sounds a different chorus—the hoarse cries of the vulture and the hyenas of the battlefield. Ten thousand **tarpaulins** guaranteed up to regulations! A hundred thousand kilos of bacon, cocoa powder, coffee-substitute— **c.o.d.**, immediate delivery! Hand grenades, lathes, cartridge pouches, marriage bureaus for widows of the fallen, leather belts, **jobbers** for war orders—serious offers only! The **cannon fodder** loaded onto trains in August and September is **moldering** in the killing fields of Belgium, the Vosges, and Masurian Lakes. . ..*

*Business thrives in the ruins. Cities become piles of ruins; villages become cemeteries; countries, deserts; populations are **beggared**; churches, horse stalls. International law, treaties and alliances, the most sacred words and the highest authority have been torn in shreds. Every **sovereign** "by the grace of God" is called a rogue and lying scoundrel by his cousin on the other side. Every diplomat is a cunning rascal to his colleagues in the other party. Every government sees every other as dooming its own people and worthy only of universal contempt. There are food riots in Venice, in Lisbon, Moscow, Singapore. There is plague in Russia, and misery and despair everywhere.*

*Violated, dishonored, wading in blood, dripping filth—there stands **bourgeois society**. This is it. Not all spic and span and moral, with pretense to culture, philosophy, ethics, order, peace, and the rule of law—but the **ravening** beast, the **witches' sabbath** of anarchy, a plague to culture and humanity. Thus [bourgeois society] reveals itself in its true, its naked form.*

*In the midst of this witches' sabbath a catastrophe of world-historical proportions has happened: International Social Democracy has **capitulated**. To deceive ourselves about it, to cover it up, would be the most foolish, the most fatal thing the **proletariat** could do. . . . The fall of the socialist proletariat in the present world war is unprecedented. It is a misfortune for humanity. But socialism will be lost only if the international proletariat fails to measure the depth of this fall, if it refuses to learn from it. . . .*

[Luxemburg recounts a forty-five-year history of the labor movement and suggests that by joining the war effort workers have given up any gains they made over the past years..]

*And what did **we** in Germany experience when **the great historical test** came? The most precipitous fall, the most violent collapse. Nowhere has the organization of the proletariat been **yoked** so com-*

Prosaic: Dull.

Tarpaulins: Waterproofed canvas coverings.

c.o.d.: Cash on delivery.

Jobbers: A person who buys merchandise from manufacturers to sell to another firm–in this case to the government.

Cannon fodder: Soldiers that are expected to be killed in battle.

Moldering: Decaying.

Beggared: Made poor.

Sovereign: Ruler.

Bourgeois society: Business owners; the class that Luxemburg thought the workers must fight in a revolution.

Ravening: Greedily waiting impatiently to eat.

Witches' sabbath: A meeting of witches.

Capitulated: Surrendered; given in.

Proletariat: Workers.

We: Proletariat workers; the working class.

The great historical test: The beginning of World War I.

Yoked: Laboring under conditions that allow no worker control.

*pletely to the service of **imperialism**. . . . Nowhere is the press so hob-bled, public opinion so stifled, the economic and political class strug-gle of the working class so totally surrendered as in Germany. . . .*

*One thing is certain. The world war is a turning point. It is fool-ish and mad to imagine that we need only survive the war, like a rab-bit waiting out the storm under a bush, in order to fall happily back into the old routine once it is over. The world war has altered the con-ditions of **our struggle** struggle and, most of all, it has changed us. Not that the **basic law of capitalist development**, the life-and-death war between capital and labor, will experience any **amelioration**. But now, in the midst of the war, the masks are falling and the old famil-iar visages smirk at us. The tempo of development has received a mighty jolt from the eruption of the volcano of imperialism. The vio-lence of the conflicts in the bosom of society, the enormousness of the tasks that tower up before the socialist proletariat—these make everything that has transpired in the history of the workers' move-ment seem a pleasant **idyll**.*

*Historically, this war was **ordained** to thrust forward the cause of the proletariat. . . . It was ordained to drive the German proletariat to the pinnacle of the nation and thereby begin to organize the interna-tional and universal conflict between capital and labor for political power within the state. . . .*

The official Handbook for Social-Democratic Voters *(1911), for the last Reichstag election, says on p. 42 concerning the expected world war:*

> *Do our rulers and ruling classes expect the peoples to permit this awful thing? Will not a cry of horror, of scorn, of outrage not seize the peoples and cause them to put an end to this murder? Will they not ask: For whom? what's it all for? Are we mentally disturbed to be treated this way, to allow ourselves to be so treated? He who is calmly convinced of the probability of a great European war can come to no other conclusion than the following: The next European war will be such a desperate gamble as the world has never seen. In all probability it will be the last war.*

[Luxemburg quotes several more socialist leaders who implore workers to resist war.]

Even a week before the outbreak of war, on July 26, 1914, Ger-man socialist party newspapers wrote:

Imperialism: A nation's quest to dominate other nations.

Our struggle: The socialist cause.

Basic law of capitalist development: Socialists believed that the capitalist economic system (that of privately owned means of production and distribution) would ultimately fail when workers revolted against the owners of the means of production and distribution.

Amelioration: Improvement.

Idyll: An easy experience.

Ordained: Destined.

*We are not marionettes. We combat with all our energy a system that makes men into will-less tools of blind circumstance, this capitalism that seeks to transform a Europe thirsting for peace into a steaming slaughterhouse. If destruction has its way, if the united will to peace of the German, the international proletariat, which will make itself known in powerful demonstrations in the coming days, if the world war cannot be fended off, then at least this should be the last war, it should become the **Goetterdaemmerung** of capitalism. (Frankfurter Volksstimme)*

Then on July 30, 1914, the central **organ** of German Social Democracy stated:

The socialist proletariat rejects any responsibility for the events being brought about by a blinded, a maddened ruling class. Let it be known that a new life shall bloom from the ruins. All responsibility falls to the wielders of power today! It is "to be or not to be!" "World-history is the world-court!"

And then came the unheard of, the unprecedented, the **4th of August 1914.**

Did it have to come? An event of this scope is certainly no game of chance. It must have deep and wide-reaching objective causes. . . .

Friedrich Engels *once said: "Bourgeois society stands at the crossroads, either transition to socialism or regression into barbarism." What does "regression into barbarism" mean to our lofty European civilization? Until now, we have all probably read and repeated these words thoughtlessly, without suspecting their fearsome seriousness. A look around us at this moment shows what the regression of bourgeois society into barbarism means. This world war is a regression into barbarism. The triumph of imperialism leads to the annihilation of civilization. At first, this happens sporadically for the duration of a modern war, but then when the period of unlimited wars begins it progresses toward its inevitable consequences. Today, we face the choice exactly as Friedrich Engels foresaw it a generation ago: either the triumph of imperialism and the collapse of all civilization as in ancient Rome, depopulation, desolation, degeneration—a great cemetery. Or the victory of socialism, that means the conscious active struggle of the international proletariat against imperialism and its method of war. . . . The future of civilization and humanity depends*

Goetterdaemmerung: Literally, this means the "twilight of the gods," but here it meant "the undoing of capitalism."

Organ: Group that is part of a larger organization.

4th of August 1914: The date the war began.

Friedrich Engels: (1820-1895) A famous German socialist.

on whether or not the proletariat resolves manfully to **throw its revolutionary broadsword into the scales** In this war imperialism has won. Its bloody sword of **genocide** has brutally tilted the scale toward the abyss of misery. The only compensation for all the misery and all the shame would be if we learn from the war how the proletariat can seize mastery of its own destiny and escape the role of the **lackey** to the ruling classes. . ..

Now, millions of proletarians of all **tongues** fall upon the field of dishonor. . .. This, too, we are not spared. We are like the Jews that Moses led through the desert. But we are not lost, and we will be victorious if we have not unlearned how to learn. And if the present leaders of the proletariat, the Social Democrats, do not understand how to learn, then they will go under "to make room for people capable of dealing with a new world."

The Junius Pamphlet

Excerpt from Chapter 8

The war means ruin for all the **belligerents**, although more so for the defeated. On the day after the concluding of peace, preparations for a new world war will be begun under the leadership of England in order to throw off the yoke of Prusso-German militarism burdening Europe and the Near East. A German victory would be only a prelude to a soon-to-follow second world war; and this would be the signal for a new, feverish arms race as well as the unleashing of the blackest reaction in all countries, but first and foremost in Germany itself.

On the other hand, an Anglo-French victory would most probably lead to the loss of at least some German colonies, as well as Alsace-Lorraine. Quite certain would be the bankruptcy of German imperialism on the world stage. But that also means the **partition** of Austria-Hungary and the total **liquidation** of Turkey. The fall of such **arch-reactionary** creatures as these two states is wholly in keeping with the demands of progressive development. [But] the fall of the **Habsburg monarchy** as well as Turkey, in the concrete situation of world politics, can have no other effect than to put their peoples **in pawn** to Russia, England, France, and Italy. Add to this grandiose redrawing of the world map power shifts in the Balkans and the Mediterranean and a further one in Asia. The liquidation of Persia and a new dismemberment of China will inevitably follow.

Throw its revolutionary broadsword into the scales: Begin a revolution.

Genocide: Deliberate killing of a group of people.

Lackey: Servant, follower.

Tongues: Nationalities.

Belligerents: All countries engaged in the war.

Partition: Division into separate parts.

Liquidation: Elimination.

Arch-reactionary: Extremely conservative; very much opposed to progress.

Habsburg monarchy: The German royal family that held power from the eleventh century; also spelled Hapsburg.

In pawn: In the position of being used to further the purposes of a more powerful nation.

In the wake [of these changes] the English-Russian, as well as the English-Japanese, conflict will move into the foreground of world politics. And directly upon the liquidation of this world war, these [conflicts] may lead to a new world war, perhaps over Constantinople, and would certainly make it likely. Thus, from this side, too, [an Anglo-French] victory would lead to a new feverish armaments race among all the states—with defeated Germany obviously in the forefront. An era of unalloyed militarism and reaction would dominate all Europe with a new world war as its ultimate goal.

Thus proletarian policy is locked in a dilemma when trying to decide on which side it ought to intervene, which side represents progress and democracy in this war. In these circumstances, and from the perspective of international politics as a whole, victory or defeat, in political as well as economic terms, comes down to a hopeless choice between two kinds of beatings for the European working classes. Therefore, it is nothing but fatal madness when the French socialists imagine that the military defeat of Germany will strike a blow at the head of militarism and imperialism and thereby pave the way for peaceful democracy in the world. Imperialism and its servant, militarism, will calculate their profits from every victory and every defeat in this war—except in one case: if the international proletariat intervenes in a revolutionary way and puts an end to such calculations.

What happened next . . .

From jail in 1916, Luxemburg and others founded the Spartacus League, a group dedicated to starting a socialist revolution. Through her writings in the group's newspaper, *The Red Flag*, Luxemburg tried to inspire the starving masses to rebel. Though the Spartacus League never started a revolution, Luxemburg continued her efforts after her release from jail in 1918. With Karl Liebknecht (1871–1919) and others from the Spartacus League, Luxemburg helped to form the German Communist Party. After the German defeat in World War I, the German Communist Party criticized the new German government and called for a complete stoppage of work, hoping that this would incite a revolution of the people and bring about the establishment of a humane government. The German Communist Party failed in its attempt to seize power in 1919, and the German government ordered Luxemburg and Liebknecht to be arrested. The two were arrested on January 15 and were also badly beaten. Luxemburg was then shot and her body dumped in Berlin's Landwehr canal. Liebknecht was also killed, and a few weeks later so was Luxemburg's lover, Leo Jogiches.

Did you know . . .

- Although Rosa Luxemburg was Jewish, she rejected her Jewish culture and assimilated (blended) into Christian society. She developed a strong anti-Semitism (hostility toward Jews) in her later years.

- Luxemburg thought that revolution should be a creation of popular will, not of violence, as was the case in Russia in 1917.

- Although Luxemburg failed to start the revolution she had envisioned, her work is well remembered and praised by modern-day socialists.

- The German government in 1919 was called the Weimar Republic. Led by Friedrich Ebert, it viewed Luxemburg's ideas as dangerously radical.

For More Information

Books

Abraham, Richard. *Rosa Luxemburg: A Life for the International*. Oxford: Berg, 1989.

Ettinger, Elbieta. *Rosa Luxemburg: A Life*. Boston: Beacon Press, 1986.

Heyman, Neil M. *World War I*. Westport, CT: Greenwood Press, 1997.

Sommerville, Donald. *World War I: History of Warfare*. Austin, TX: Raintree Steck-Vaughn, 1999.

Winter, Jay, and Blaine Baggett. *The Great War and the Shaping of the 20th Century*. New York: Penguin Studio, 1996.

Web sites

"The Great War and the Shaping of the 20th Century." [Online] http://www.pbs.org/greatwar (accessed February 2001).

Luxemburg, Rosa. *The Junius Pamphlet.* Translated by Dave Hollis. [Online] http://www.marxists.org/archive/luxembur/works/1915/04.htm (accessed April 2001).

The Rosa Luxemburg Internet Archive. [Online] http://www.marxists.org/archive/luxembur/index.htm (accessed May 2001).

The Russian Revolution

*Telegrams from the American Consulate in Moscow and
Petrograd to the U.S. Secretary of State, March 20, 1917*

**Reprinted from the *Hanover Historical Texts Project*, available
online at http://history.hanover.edu/texts/tel3.html and
http://history.hanover.edu/texts/tel2.html
Scanned and edited by David Traill**

Every combatant country suffered during World War I. To
cope with the numerous deaths and massive destruction of
World War I, governments had to balance the needs on the
homefront with the demands of the battlefront. Governments
created new agencies to feed and supply their military and
their masses. Because Germany was already heavily industrial-
ized and the German government enjoyed very direct control
over civil life, Germany was the quickest to make the transition to a wartime economy. The German government established a War Raw Materials Division of the Ministry of War,
under the charge of prominent businessman Walther
Rathenau. Rathenau quickly organized and coordinated the
efforts of German companies to produce all the materials necessary to supply German forces. Britain and France had far
fewer factories and little heavy industry, and thus they were
less prepared to produce the guns, shells, and heavy machin-
ery vital to the war effort. Their governments also exercised
less direct control over the people, making the coordination of
production less efficient than in Germany. The Allied countries, however, had free access to the seas and were able to

"I have had to defend
the American eagle on
the top of the building,
as it was believed to be a
German eagle and the
crowd intended to tear it
down until I explained in
Russian the difference
between the American
and German eagle."

*From the American Consulate
in Petrograd to the U.S.
Secretary of State*

import many of their war materials from overseas, especially from the United States.

Russia, however, had great difficulty converting to a wartime economy. Hundreds of miles of Russia's border were exposed to attacks by the German army, and Russia had entered the war with far fewer munitions than it required. As a result, the Russians suffered astonishing defeats against the better-equipped German forces. Russia was also geographically isolated from its French allies, so it couldn't rely on quick or easy access to aid. Russia therefore had to rely solely on its own industrial and agricultural production. The Russians were able to build more munitions and grow more food, but the country's inadequate transportation system left piles of supplies waiting at distribution points, far from where they were needed. Workers suffered terrible working conditions in jobs they were forced to perform for their country. To make matters worse, as food supplies grew scarce, people had to wait for hours in long lines for bread and coal. Many Russians faced starvation. These difficulties triggered nationwide strikes and protests by March 1917.

The protests for more food began in Petrograd (formerly St. Petersburg) and quickly spread. To control the massive protests and strikes in the major cities of Petrograd and Moscow, the government ordered its loyal mounted troops, the Cossacks, to break up the protests, but neither the Cossacks nor members of the army were willing to repress the people any longer. In fact, many men from the army "switched sides," joining with the people in their protest against the government. The soldiers had demands of their own: They too wanted food, but they also wanted an end to the war. Telegrams sent during the early uprisings capture the confusion of the time and detail the hardships that led to revolution in Russia.

Things to remember while reading the telegrams from the American Consulate:

- When reading about the Russian Revolution you will often need to check the style of calendar the author is using. At the time of the revolution, Russia used the Julian calendar; this "Old Style" calendar was twelve days behind the Western, or Georgian, calendar that is used today. Therefore, the "February Revolution" actually began in March of the Western calendar. All dates, unless otherwise noted, are according to the Western calendar in this book.

- Many separate events escalated the tensions that eventually caused the revolution. On International Women's Day, (February 23, 1917, of the Julian "Old Style" calendar, March 8, 1917, of the Western, or Georgian, calendar), a large crowd of women protested about the food shortages. The next day 200,000 workers went on strike in Petrograd. Loyal military troops shot into crowds of strikers and killed more than 300 protestors two days later.

- Even though thousands of workers were pleading for food and striking, the Russian government refused to make any concessions to the protestors.

- The loyalty of the army was the only thing that could save the monarchy of Russia or win the revolution for the masses. When the soldiers in Petrograd barracks learned that soldiers had opened fire on the protestors, more than 100 grabbed guns and rushed to protect the protestors from the cruelty of their peers. The next day, more than 25,000 soldiers mutinied (rebelled against authority) and joined the revolution, handing out guns to the masses.

- The armed soldiers helped the masses capture important government buildings, railway stations, and telegraph exchanges.

Excerpt from a Telegram from the American Consulate in Moscow to the U.S. Secretary of State

CONFIDENTIAL.

No. 1019 American Consulate General,

Moscow, Russia, March 20th, 1917.

Subject. The political and economical situation in Moscow.

The Honorable

The Secretary of State,

Washington, D. C.

Sir:

For the information, and as of interest to the Department in following the great revolution now in progress in Russia, there are enclosed herewith the originals and translations of the Moscow papers giving a full description of the matter. This same information has been sent the Embassy together with full accounts of the situation.

It will be observed that the papers are allowed only to publish news favoring the revolutionary party.

There is further enclosed a memorandum on the situation prepared by Mr. David B. Macgowan, the Vice Consul at this post. It is of interest as showing the other phase of the situation.

At the present writing the street cars are all running, and life has assumed its normal course. There is an undercurrent of unrest, however, and the shortage of food supplies tends to augment the discontent. Long bread lines stretching for blocks may be seen on every street awaiting often to be told that there is none left. The daily allowance is one funt or nine tenths of a pound. To obtain this one must stand in the bread lines for two or three hours, and often longer. The supply of flour is short and the revolution of the past few days has diminished even this. It is known that the Jews have cornered large quantities and are holding it for higher prices.

*Prices of all articles of necessity are rapidly rising. It is difficult to give a table showing same as the figures given out are purely fictitious, each shop charging what they can get. Flour, for instance cannot be bought at all. There is none for sale in the city. Meat is practically unobtainable, and then only three days in the week. Milk, eggs, flour, bread, and meat will soon be sold only **by card.***

The city is thronged with refugees and houses are unobtainable even at exorbitant prices.

As the Consulate General is furnishing the Embassy daily with full information in regard to the political situation it is presumed that, through this source, the Department is kept thoroughly advised of the situation.

I have the honor to be, Sir,

Your obedient servant,

[signature indecipherable]

American Consul in Charge.

Enclosures:

Newspaper translations.

Memorandum Mr. Macgowan.

MEMORANDUM.

Moscow, Russia, March 19, 1917.

*The **coup d'etat**, a stage of the uncompleted revolution, executed by revolutionary workingmen and soldiers, too recently recruited to have acquired discipline or to have lost touch with their late companions in field and factory, has **whetted** already keen appetites for land, social reorganization and autonomy or independence. The **Imperial Duma**, declared dissolved, it would seem, in lighthearted confidence*

By card: A ration card must be presented to obtain certain goods.

Coup d'etat: An overthrow of a government.

Whetted: Stimulated.

Imperial Duma: Government.

that the bread riots could be ended with machine guns, if the Duma were safely out of the way, neither initiated the crisis nor is certain to guide its further development. Discipline was shaken, perhaps irreparably, when soldiers disarmed their officers. In the absence of popular interest in the war . . . it is to be feared that troops at the front will slip away from their commands and return to take part in the **carnival of liberty**, which to most of them means seizing the large estates for themselves. The workingmen are demanding an immediate **Constituent Assembly** and there is a tendency not to return to factory and barrack, nor to yield newly acquired weapons, until the political and social reorganization are assured. There is imminent danger of a **debacle**. Thus, Thursday night a former Deputy of the Imperial Duma returned from Petrograd to Moscow. The train, including the first class car in which the Deputy had reserved a compartment, was seized by **soldiers under arms**. He demanded what they were doing in the first class car. The soldiers answered they were going to their native villages to see their relatives. He asked if they had **leave of absence** and was told "No." They were going "just so." Asked when they would return to their regiments, they said the war might be over before they had to return. Soldiers are represented in the powerful Councils of Workingmen's Delegates; they retain their rifles and they are to have votes. If the soldiers at the front should seize trains and return, as happened after the **Russo-Japanese war**, there is reason to fear that the excesses then committed will be a foretaste of worse to come. In these circumstances the Anglo-French offensive, vigorously and successfully pushed to the conviction of the wavering Russian troops that the war can be fought to an end so that there will be no need to abandon it in order to share in the "**expropriation**" of the land, is the main hope for Russia, as respects not only the hopeful **prosecution** of the war, but as respects the peaceful evolution of political and social order. Already about ten days have been lost for preparation of munitions, and it is to be feared that, even if they return to work, the munitions workers will have little heart for the business. Thus, with minds distracted more than ever by domestic events, handicapped and disorganized as never before, it can hardly be expected that a blow delivered now or in the near future by the Germans would meet with effective resistance, unless the Western Powers should create an effective diversion. . . .

Reaction, violent as the revolutionary blow was violent, is sure to come and it will enlist powerful property interests. Indications thus point to a **protracted** class struggle.

D.B.M.

Carnival of liberty: The thrilling period after the successful coup d'etat that overthrew the Russian government.

Constituent Assembly: A legal body formed to make or change a constitution.

Debacle: Complete collapse of order.

Soldiers under arms: Soldiers with guns drawn.

Leave of absence: Official permission.

Russo-Japanese war: Russian war with Japan over Manchuria (1904–05).

Expropriation: Transfer of ownership to oneself.

Prosecution: Pursuing until completion.

Protracted: Lengthy.

D.B.M.: Initials of David B. Macgowan, Vice consul at the American Consulate in Moscow.

Telegram from the American Consulate in Petrograd to the U.S. Secretary of State

No. 274

AMERICAN CONSULATE

Petrograd, Russia, March 20, 1917

(Confidential)

SUBJECT: Revolutionary Movement in Petrograd.

THE HONORABLE

The Secretary Of State

WASHINGTON

SIR:

I have the honor to report that as a result of serious economic, political, and military disturbances, the government of this city and district has been completely assumed by an Executive Committee of the Imperial Duma at least for the time being.

On the beginning of the week of March 4th, a shortage of black bread was noticeable. This at once caused unrest among the laboring classes. All other prime necessities within the means of the working classes had already gradually disappeared as the winter advanced: meat, sugar, white flour, buckwheat, potatoes. Fish, fowls, eggs, milk, cheese, and butter, had for a long time been so expensive that they were only within the means of the very well-to-do classes. The unrest first took visible form in the outskirts and factory districts of the city Wednesday, March 7th, when the workmen struck after the dinner hour and met in groups to discuss the situation.

*The next day, Thursday March 8th, there were spontaneous isolated demonstrations. In many places, a few of the working class, mostly women, tired of waiting in the bread lines in the severe cold began to cry, "Give us bread." These groups were immediately dispersed by large detachments of mounted police and **Cossacks**.*

March 9th, large crowds of women marched to the Kazan Cathedral (opposite the Consulate) with bared heads, still crying for bread and shouting to the police "Give us bread and we will go to work." This crowd was peaceable and was dispersed.

Saturday morning the crowds, composed of working men and students visibly with a serious purpose, came from all districts to the

Cossacks: Russian cavalry.

*center of the city. Besides calling for bread, these crowds shouted "Down with the Government," "Down with the **Romanoffs**," and occasionally "Down with the War." The mounted police endeavored to drive the mobs from the Nevsky, the main street, but resistence [sic] was made and barracades [sic] built on the side streets. The police withdrew after firing on and charging the crowds with whips without success. Their place was taken by infantry who fraternized with the people. Announcement was made by the police that after 6 o'clock that day, all groups of persons would be fired upon. The crowds did not disperse, and street battles took place, especially on the Nevsky, resulting in great loss of life.*

At this time the infantry and cossacks refused to fire on the crowds or to charge them. Towards evening a detachment of cossacks actually charged and dispersed a body of mounted police.

*Sunday, when it became known that [Czar Nicholas] had **prorogued the Duma** and that it had refused to recognize this order, there was disorganized and sporadic fighting all over the city, with heavy loss of life. The unmounted police were withdrawn from the streets. Many regiments which had been locked in their barracks mutinied, during the night, killed some of their officers, and marched to defend the Duma, which was still sitting. By Monday the disorganized riots developed into a systematic revolutionary movement on the part of the working men and the constantly growing numbers of mutinied troops, to capture the city of Petrograd. The fighting moved rapidly across the city from the Duma as a center, so that by Monday night, only isolated houses and public buildings, upon which machine guns were mounted, were held by the police and the few remaining loyal troops. At midnight the Duma had announced that it had taken the government into its own hands and had formed an Executive Committee to be the head of the temporary government.*

Tuesday and Wednesday the fighting was confined to volleys from machine guns fired by the police from the isolated house tops, public buildings and churches, and the return fire by the soldiers, such fighting continuing until all police were taken. Violence necessary in arresting government, army and police officials, took place at this time.

During these two days the fighting around the Consulate was severe, and on several occasions it seemed as if nothing could save the Singer Building from total demolition. Machine guns were presumably being operated from points of advantage in this building by police agents, as well as from neighboring buildings, the revolutionists replying with volleys from their rifles and machine guns mounted in automobiles.

Romanoffs: The Russian royal family.

Prorogued the Duma: Canceled the Russian legislative assembly.

At 4:30 o'clock Monday afternoon troops, always without officers, entered the building. All the business offices in it had been deserted early in the day, except the Consulate. When the soldiers reached the third floor they were shown the location of the Consulate by one of the staff. They insisted on seeing the balconies of the Consulate, and several soldiers, with members of the Consulate staff entered the Consulate and satisfied themselves that no machine guns were located there. No damage was done in the Consulate, but other offices and the building itself were considerably injured.

Notice was given that kerosene would be poured on the building and burned. At 5:30 o'clock the Consulate was closed after everything of importance had been placed in the safe and notices posted on all the doors, stating that the nature of the office was foreign and contained only property of the United States Government. The staff left the building under heavy fire and with a guard.

At 6:30 o'clock, when the firing had ceased, it was arranged to have a Consulate employee constantly on duty, day and night. This alone saved the Consulate from being violated, for Tuesday and Wednesday there was no order in the city and the Singer building was visited five times by armed soldiers, many of whom were intoxicated, looking for weapons.

A military guard has now been furnished the Consulate and the office is intact, and safe for the present at least. The fact that the Consulate is not in a separate building owned by the American Government is particularly unfortunate in this city, there the question of protection of Americana is so apt to arise and where prejudices against firms located in the same building endangers the Consulate and the lives of the staff.

The Singer building has been under suspicion since the beginning of the war as being German, the masses believing the Singer Company to be a German corporation.

I have had to defend the American eagle on the top of the building, as it was believed to be a German eagle and the crowd intended to tear it down until I explained in Russian the difference between the American and German eagle.

The Consulate is keeping in touch with the members of the American colony, none of whom up to the present have been injured. As the Consulate is not at all suitable for housing purposes, having no kitchen, bath or sleeping accommodations, I have notified the members of the Colony that in case they are turned out of their homes or hotels or have to leave for protection, they may come to my home, which is centrally located, where I could protect them and make them fairly comfortable.

I shall make only a limited report of observations on the political situation leading up to the economic situation in this district. It being supposed the Embassy has already cabled a report in the matter.

Immediately following the assumption of national authority by the Executive Committee of the Duma, the Council of Workmens' Deputies challenged its exclusive authority. This council is a body which existed secretly during the old regime and represented the revolutionary workmen. Spontaneously a third authority appeared in the Council of Soldiers' Deputies which soon merged with the workmens' council under the name of the Council of Workmen's Soldiers' Deputies.

Tuesday, Wednesday, and Thursday, (the 13th, 14th, and 15th,) were, up to the present, the most critical times of the revolution, when there was immediate danger of civil war in Petrograd between the Duma and the Council of Workmens' and Soldiers' Deputies. This crisis passed however, when, late on Thursday afternoon, a provisional agreement was reached. This agreement was based on a temporary ministry chosen from the members of the Duma with a political program of eight points:

1. *Immediate political **amnesty**.*

2. *Immediate freedom of press, speech, meeting, the right to strike; these rights to be extended to soldiers insofar as compatible with military organization.*

3. *Immediate abolition of all **caste**, religious, and race difficulties.*

4. *Immediate preparation for a constitutional convention to determine the permanent form of national government.*

5. *Immediate substitution of militia with elective officers, under control of local self-governing bodies in place of the old police system.*

6. *Election to local self-governing bodies by universal direct, equal, and secret suffrage.*

7. *Retention of arms by revolutionary soldiery, the soldiery not to be removed from Petrograd.*

8. *Retention of strict military discipline during actual service with full civil freedom to soldiers when not on duty.*

Amnesty: A pardon granted by a government for political wrongdoings.

Caste: Social classes.

On the 15th of March the Emperor abdicated for himself in favor of his brother the Grand Duke Michael. On the 16th the Grand Duke Michael declined the throne unless it should be offered him by the Constitutional Convention. This again averted further civil war as it put all parties in agreement to await the Constitutional Convention.

The old police which was maintained by the national government as a part of the Ministry of the Interior, has been replaced by the City Militia, a volunteer organization under the **auspice** of the National Duma and the Board of Aldermen. It is now maintaining order throughout the city and cooperating with the **Commissariats** in the various wards. The Commissariats are under the control of the Council of Workmen's and Soldiers' Deputies, which still sits in conjunction with the National Duma.

Passport regulations for foreigners have not been changed and are controlled by a new Gradonatchalnik (Chief of City or Chief of Police) who is now, as formerly, dependent on the Ministry of the Interior.

A new Mayor has been chosen by the Aldermen. He is attempting to control and improve the local food supply which is again the danger point as at the beginning of the revolution. All necessities have to be brought to Petrograd from the provinces and a serious food shortage now exists. If it is not relieved at once it will cause further serious disorders capable of developing into new revolutionary movements with greater socialistic tendencies than heretofore.

Today, March 20th, for the first time in ten days, a very few electric street cars are running but not enough to constitute a resumption of the service. The workmen have not returned to the factories as was hoped.

I have the etc. ["the honor to be, Sir, Your obedient servant," is crossed out]

North Winship [signature]

["American Consul." is crossed out]

Auspice: Protection, support.

Commissariats: A government department in Russia.

What happened next . . .

By mid-March 1917 the people of Russia were in all-out revolt against the government. Convinced by his generals that

Boy Scouts of America—Unite!

The war effort permeated everyone's life. Through appeals to various youth organizations, the U.S. government even asked children to contribute. For example, President Woodrow Wilson called on the Boy Scouts of America for help in distributing patriotic pamphlets to every U.S. home. The Boy Scouts of America published *Boys' Life*, one of the nation's most widely read youth magazines. It had a vast network of young boys who were interested in becoming good citizens; and during World War I, being a good citizen meant serving the war effort. The following excerpt from a Boy Scouts of America pamphlet shows how the leadership rallied their scouts into service on the home front to keep the United States safe from the type of internal conflict that was plaguing Russia.

To the Members of the Boy Scouts of America!

Attention, Scouts! We are again called upon to do active service for our country! Every one of the 285,661 Scouts and 76,957 Scout Officials has been summoned by President Woodrow Wilson, Commander-in-Chief of the Army and Navy, to serve as a dispatch bearer from the Government at Washington to the American people all over the country. The prompt, enthusiastic, and hearty response of every one of us has been pledged by our [Scout] President, Mr. Livingstone. Our splendid record of accomplishments in war activities promises full success in this new job.

This patriotic service will be rendered under the slogan: "EVERY SCOUT TO BOOST AMERICA" AS A GOVERNMENT DISPATCH BEARER. The World War is for liberty and democracy.. . .

As a democracy, our country faces great danger—not so much from submarines, battleships and armies, because, thanks to our allies, our enemies have apparently little chance of reaching our shores.

Our danger is from within. Our enemies have representatives everywhere;

there was nothing he could do to stop the revolution, Czar Nicholas abdicated (gave up the throne) on March 15. His replacement, his brother Grand Duke Michael, quickly appointed a provisional (temporary) government. The provisional government tried to bring peace and reform to the country, but it was unwilling to do the one thing that might save it: end Russia's involvement in the war. And so the revolt continued. Peasants took over land for themselves, and soldiers by the thousands deserted the army. The peasants, workers, and soldiers were all encouraged in their actions by a group they tell lies; they mispresent the truth; they deceive our own people; they are a real menace to our country.

Already we have seen how poor Russia has been made to suffer because her people do not know the truth. Representatives of the enemy have been very effective in their deceitful efforts to make trouble for the Government.

Fortunately here in America our people are better educated—they want the truth. Our President recognized the justice and wisdom of this demand when in the early stages of the war he created the Committee on Public Information. He knew that the Government would need the confidence, enthusiasm and willing service of every man and woman, every boy and girl in the nation. He knew that the only possible way to create a genuine feeling of partnership between the people and its representatives in Washington was to take the people into his confidence by full, frank statements concerning the reasons for our entering the war, the various steps taken during the war and the ultimate aims of the war.

Neither the President as Commander-in-Chief, nor our army and navy by land and sea, can alone win the war. At this moment the best defense that America has is an enlightened and loyal citizenship.. . .

Here is where our service begins. We are to help spread the facts about America and America's part in the World War. We are to fight lies with truth.

We are to help create public opinion "just as effective in helping to bring victory as ships and guns," to stir patriotism, the great force behind the ships and guns. Isn't that a challenge for every loyal Scout?. . .

Under the direction of our leaders, the Boy Scouts of America are to serve as an intelligence division of the citizens' army, always prepared and alert to respond to any call which may come from the President of the United States and the Committee on Public Information at Washington.

Excerpt from a pamphlet entitled Committee on Public Information, Boy Scouts of America, 1917. Available online at http://longman.awl.com/history/primarysource_22_1.htm (accessed April 2001).

of radicals known as "soviets," a word that means "representatives of the workers." The most radical of the "soviets" were known as Bolsheviks, and they took the revolution to the next stage in the fall of 1917.

When the provisional government ordered an ill-advised military offensive in the summer of 1917, the Russians were driven decisively back. The failed Russian offensive had two results: It furthered the disintegration of the military, and it spurred the Bolsheviks to action. In the north, German forces overran the Russian province of Latvia and controlled access to the Baltic Sea. In the cities of Petrograd and Moscow in early November 1917, Bolshevik leaders Vladimir Ilich Lenin and Leon Trotsky masterminded a swift action that put control of the government in their hands. The Russian Revolution was over, and the Bolsheviks—who promised to end the war and put control of Russian land and industry into the hands of the people—had won.

One of the first actions of the new Russian government was to ask Germany for an armistice, a truce ending the war. Negotiator Trotsky asked that his country, Russia, pay no price for its defeat, but the Germans set a high price on the deal: They wanted independence for many of the states and provinces within the Russian empire. The Bolsheviks initially refused, but ongoing German military attacks all along the Russian frontier finally forced the Russians to give in. When Trotsky signed the Treaty of Brest-Litovsk on March 3, 1918, Russia gave away vast tracts of Russian territory, including Estonia, Latvia, Lithuania, Belarus, and the Ukraine (all of which gained their independence). Russia also lost 25 percent of its population and 75 percent of its coal and iron resources.

The peace concessions and the structure of the new Communist government upset Russian citizens and started a civil war that would last until 1921 and lead to the establishment of the Soviet Union. During the civil war, the Red Army fought against the anticommunist Whites. By 1921, a hundred thousand Russians had died in the civil war and another two million had left the country.

Did you know . . .

- Italy and Austria-Hungary could have suffered an economic collapse just as Russia did in 1917. But Austria-Hungary received generous supplies of German munitions, and Italy's allies provided her with needed food, coal, industrial raw materials, and almost three billion dollars in loans, according to Paul Kennedy in *The Rise and Fall of the Great Powers*.

- Although French soldiers mutinied in 1917, the situation in France was not nearly as desperate as the circumstances in Russia, Italy, or Austria-Hungary. France avoided revolution in part because the French people had a strong belief in national unity, a desire to rid their countryside of Germans, and a steady supply of imports from Great Britain and America. Soon after the 1917 mutiny, for example, a fresh supply of bread arrived from America, which helped calm the hungry masses.

- Strikes in both Great Britain and France subsided at the end of 1917.

- Strikes escalated in Germany in 1917 and 1918. Members of the Socialist Party and the Spartacus League made independent calls for the end of the war. By 1918, Germany suffered nationwide strikes and military mutinies.

For More Information

Books

Heyman, Neil M. *World War I*. Westport, CT: Greenwood Press, 1997.

Kennedy, Paul. *The Rise and Fall of the Great Powers*. New York: Random House, 1987.

Paxton, John. *Companion to Russian History*. New York: Facts on File, 1983.

Sommerville, Donald. *World War I: History of Warfare*. Austin, TX: Raintree Steck-Vaughn, 1999.

Winter, Jay, and Blaine Baggett. *The Great War and the Shaping of the 20th Century*. New York: Penguin Studio, 1996.

Web sites

Traill, David, ed. "Telegram from the American Consulate in Moscow to the U.S. Secretary of State, March 20, 1917." *Hanover Historical Texts Project*. [Online] http://history.hanover.edu/texts/tel3.html (accessed April 2001).

Traill, David, ed. "Telegram from the American Consulate in Petrograd to the U.S. Secretary of State, March 20, 1917." *Hanover Historical Texts Project*. [Online] http://history.hanover.edu/texts/tel2.html (accessed April 2001).

Text Credits

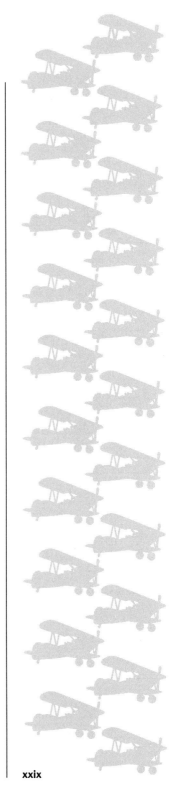

Following is a list of the copyright holders who have granted us permission to reproduce excerpts from primary source documents in *World War I: Primary Sources*. Every effort has been made to trace copyright; if omissions have been made, please let us know:

Grave, Robert. From *Good-bye to All That*. Anchor Books, 1989. Copyright © 1929, 1957 by Robert Graves, renewed 1985. Reproduced by permission of the Literary Estate of Robert Graves.

Hemingway, Ernest. From *A Farewell to Arms*. Charles Scribner's Sons, 1929. Copyright 1929 Charles Scribner's Sons. Renewal copyright © 1957 Ernest Hemingway. Reproduced by permission of Charles Scribner's Sons, an imprint of Simon & Schuster Macmillan.

Junger, Ernst. From *The Storm of Steel: From the Diary of A German Storm-Troop Officer on the Western Front*. Chatto & Windus, 1929. Reproduced by permission of the Literary Estate of Ernst Junger.

Index

Bold type indicates
main entries and their page
numbers. Illustrations are
marked by (ill).